Quick and Dirty

A Compact Guide to Writing, Reading, and Research

THIRD EDITION

Fred Cooksey

Crooked Pig Press

Easthampton, Massachusetts

CROOKED PIG PRESS

116 Pleasant Street

Suite 49

Easthampton, Massachusetts 01027

413.282.8701

Manufactured in the United States of America.

For Zoe, Betsy, Mom, and Ramona

facebook.com/quickanddirty

CONTENTS

III RESEARCH AND DOCUMENTATION

Preface

Why is it called *Quick and Dirty*?

You don't hear it much anymore, but people used to say, "Just give me the quick and dirty." It meant: Tell me what I need to know efficiently and without excess explanation. That was my goal in writing this book—to give students the information they need about writing, reading, and research quickly, and in simple terms.

Acknowledgements

I would like to thank my many colleagues in the Holyoke Community College English Department who have used this book in their courses: Elizabeth Trobaugh, Lisa Mahon, Alex Wagman, Sarah Gilleman, Pat Kennedy, Frank Johnson, Petriana Monize, Michael Roberts, Sean Reagan, Ben Hersey, Michael Fournier, Ata Moharreri, Susan Krane, Susan McNitt, and—from the very rough beginning—Mike Walker. Their feedback has been essential to the continued improvement of this book.

I would also like to thank Kiersten Delfox-Conrad, of Langley (VA) High School, for her sage advice and enthusiastic support.

Additional thanks to my friends, colleagues, and former students who saved me from substantial embarrassment by proofreading multiple chapters of this book: Elizabeth Choi, Laura D'Angelo, Mara Dodge, Kristin LaCasse, Sara Manau, Steve Swygert, and Chris Trubac.

Mere gratitude does not sufficiently express my appreciation for the patience and wisdom of my wife, Betsy Gillen, who has read and critiqued this book numerous times; I can always count on Betsy to identify and correct my lapses, errors, and misjudgments (in text as in life).

Finally, thanks to the many students who have offered kind words of encouragement as well as some very useful suggestions.

Fred Cooksey
July 2013

chapter 1

COLLEGE SURVIVAL

OR, WHAT *NOT* TO DO IN YOUR CLASSES

Only the educated are free.

~ Epictetus

The more we learn the more we realize how little we know.

~ R. Buckminster Fuller

What does a college degree mean in America today?

A piece of paper.

That's how students often talk about it, and that—in many ways—is how many employers view it.

Particularly in the world of work, a college degree means that you are able to complete a variety of time-consuming, sometimes demanding, and sometimes tedious tasks. Some of those tasks will require you to apply every ounce of your intelligence, while others will call only on your ability to memorize trivial information that you will probably forget within a matter of hours.

Finishing college may or may not make you smarter, but it will certainly prove that you have discipline. That's why employers want people with college degrees. When you complete a degree, it communicates to potential employers, "I am able to complete many tasks, even when some of them are not terribly interesting to me personally."

And that's an admirable personal quality, one that you will find useful in any number of real-life situations.

However. This is a big However. What I just described is what college "represents" in our world. That doesn't mean that college can't—and shouldn't—be much more. It *should* make you a deeper and more analytical thinker. It *should* expose you to new ideas that cause you to rethink your understanding of the world. It *should* allow you to approach intellectual and practical problems in more creative and productive ways. It *should* make you a better citizen.

As someone who believes in the ability of college to do all of those things (and more), I'm asking you to try to pursue those high-minded ideals. Avoid courses that ask you only to memorize and regurgitate information. Seek out courses that turn your intellectual world upside-down, that confuse and bewilder and challenge you.

It's worth it.

* * *

So here you are in college. Maybe you're eighteen and just out of high school. Or you took some time off (a year? twenty years?) to work, have a family. Whoever you are, if you're reading this, it's most likely because you're taking English composition (or "first-year writing," or "freshman comp"—whatever your college calls it).

It's the one course that nearly every college student in America must take. And it's a course that many students dread. But it doesn't have to be that way. Much of that dread, I believe, comes from fear—fear of red "correction" marks (like blood) all over your papers, fear of assignments and directions you don't understand.

That fear is what motivated me to write this book. My goal was to create a brief guide to the most important skills you need to start writing at the college level. For me, that begins with survival skills. Plenty of books suggest "techniques for success," but I find most of the suggestions clichéd: study hard, don't put off assignments till the last minute, take a multivitamin, etc. Instead, I'll tell you what *not* to do. It takes the form of a Top 10 list.

If nothing in this list is news to you, and you'd never dream of doing these things, please forgive me for wasting your time.

WHAT NOT TO DO IN YOUR COLLEGE CLASSES

10. Ignore the syllabus

Some students, it would seem, never bother to read the syllabus. This is a big mistake, and one that will often hurt you in the course. I know—it's annoying that every professor has different policies around absences, grading, phones, late papers, etc. But it's not so different from the real world, where one boss will be lenient and easy-going while another will be strict and demanding.

Do yourself a favor and read the syllabus closely. Your professor will be impressed if you're able to say, for example, "I know that if I turn the paper in Thursday, there will be a half-letter-grade penalty." He might even be impressed enough to grade your paper a little more generously.

9. Use email inappropriately

When you need to call or email your professor, think about the language and form you use. Far too many students send emails that look like this:

> hi, i'm in your english class and can't come to school today my mom's car is in the shop and there are no buses around here so let me know what i need to do.

Even if your professor wants you to call her by her first name, you should try to make your language and tone relatively formal. It should not read like a text to one of your friends.

> Dear Professor ________,
>
> I'm in your MWF 10-10:50 English class, and I am unable to come to school today. I will continue to read the essay that's assigned on the syllabus, but if there's anything else I should do, please let me know. Thank you very much.
>
> Sincerely,
>
> Joe Student

A few basic guidelines: Use capital letters, as you would in a paper for class. Write in complete sentences. Thank the person you're writing to. Include a "closing," e.g., Sincerely, or Kind regards, or Best. Proofread.

Finally, take the same approach to phone messages. Speak clearly, say your phone number slowly, twice, and thank the person you're calling.

8. Talk while professor is talking

Rude, disrespectful.

7. Come to class without book(s), paper, pen, etc.

Makes you look like you don't care. And maybe you don't. But that certainly won't reflect well on you when we're grading your papers, tests, etc. I could pretend that we grade everything "in a vacuum," which is to say without thinking about who you are as a person in the classroom. But that would be a lie. It's like anything else in life—you're always making an impression on the people around you. What will yours be?

6. Make excuses and/or fail to take responsibility

You'll find a whole range of humanity among your professors, but I think that many of us tend to be compassionate—at least up to a point. We want to believe you, for example, when you tell us your grandmother died and you had to go to her funeral, and we don't want to penalize your paper for lateness as a result.

But this type of scenario puts us in a difficult position. You could be lying (we've been lied to in the past, we know that much). If you are, then you're getting away with something, and getting an unfair advantage over your classmates. If you're not lying to us, then probably you deserve a break.

But here's the problem—how do we know the difference? And what about students who are too shy or private to share this kind of information with us

I often struggle with these questions. And I don't think I'm terribly consistent in how I deal with them. Sometimes I give students a break, sometimes I don't.

The lesson for you is this: If you have a legitimate emergency that affects your performance in a class, talk to your professor. He or she might not make any allowances for you, but many professors do want to know.

The other side of this lesson is this: You don't need to tell your professor about every little thing that goes wrong in your life. We don't need to know that you got a flat tire on the way to school, or that your alarm clock is broken and you can't afford to buy a new one because you just spent all your money on a new tire, or that you were throwing up all night and that's why you didn't write your paper.

5. Pack up papers and books before class is over

Rude, rude, rude. Both to the professor and your classmates. It's noisy and distracting. When you do this, you are communicating to all who can see or hear you, "I have declared this class to be finished."

Relax.

4. Come to class late / leave class early

I've been persuaded by my colleague Victor Katz, a professor of art history at my college, that lateness is a worse "crime" than simply missing class. (Most professors, by the way, do not share this view, but I find Victor's argument compelling.)

As Victor says, "Late has victims; absent does not." By this he means that when you're late (or you leave early), you interrupt class, which affects both your teacher's ability to teach and your classmates' ability to learn. It doesn't matter how quietly you come in or leave—it's distracting.

3. Ask the professor "Did I miss anything?" after an absence

Of course you missed something. You missed *class*, that time during which I attempt to teach you something *every single day*.

Rephrasing the question as "What did I miss?" is an improvement, but before you ask this, think about how you might avoid the question altogether. If the course syllabus includes a calendar of assignments, look there to see what you missed. You might also ask a classmate before or after the next class you attend; maybe you can borrow that person's notes.

If you still have questions, then go talk to the professor during office hours. But don't expect us to go over everything we did. We'll give you a brief summary of the subject(s) we covered, and then it's your responsibility to figure out how to learn that material. This is true even if you had an excellent reason for missing class. We simply can't recreate a 50- or 75-minute class for every student who's absent.

In short, try to be as self-reliant as you can. Your professors will be impressed when you can figure out the material you missed and keep up.

2. Skip required reading

More and more often, it seems, students are coming to class without having done assigned reading. Maybe you figure the professor will be "going over" that article or chapter, so there's no point in reading it in advance.

Here's the irony of this development. For the last twenty or so years, professors have been encouraged to lecture less and involve students in classroom discussions more. Many of us have moved in this direction, but now, when we try to have an actual discussion about a reading assignment, it often falls flat because half the class (or more) hasn't done the reading.

In terms of being educated, there's nothing more important than reading. Not browsing, not checking the Spark Notes, not googling a summary—just good old-fashioned reading.

1. Become disctracted / become a distraction

If you're using a phone or some other electronic device during class, you're not giving the professor—or your classmates—your full attention. I don't allow laptops in my classes, though I may have to rethink this prohibition at some point. I recognize that laptops can be beneficial in a variety of ways (note-taking, vocabulary, fact-checking, etc.), but I also know that many students aren't using them to augment what's going on in class; they're using them to *escape* what's going on in class. They're checking Facebook or Twitter or Instagram or their fantasy football leagues, shopping for shoes, applying for jobs. All fun and even useful things to do. But not during class, please.

Of course, some students will argue that if a class is boring, then what's the harm in escaping for a few minutes? But the harm is not to you—it's to me and your classmates, many of whom are aware of what you're doing and are distracted by it. This is particularly problematic with laptops because everyone behind you can see what's on your screen.

I love the Internet. I spend far too much time on it, and not much of it is well-spent, so I'm not judging you. But I am asking you to consider how your decision to entertain yourself during class may affect the people around you as well as your professor.

Even if your professor doesn't have a stated policy about phones or laptops, I would encourage you to try to be electronics-free during class. There's a lot to be said for the old-fashioned approach of taking hand-written notes and simply being fully *present* for your education.

chapter 2

READING AND CRITICAL THINKING

Too often we give students answers to remember rather than problems to solve.

~ Roger Lewin

All writing is rhetorical. This is a popular saying among English teachers. What it means is that writers are always trying to get the reader to see things their way. I'm challenging you, in this chapter, to think about how writers make rhetorical decisions that—they hope—will cause you to agree with the "world" they're presenting in their writing.

In college, you'll be asked to read three basic types of writing: informative, argumentative, and literary. The difference between informative and argumentative writing may seem obvious, but often it isn't—mainly because many writers who are trying to get you to see things their way are good at presenting their views as, seemingly, information or fact. So, even when you're reading an article or essay that appears to be plainly informative, you should be aware of how the writer may be "positioned" on a particular issue. In other words, she may have a stance or point of view that she wants you to accept.

INFORMATIVE VS. ARGUMENTATIVE WRITING

Informative Writing

- Most textbooks
- Newspaper and magazine reportage: articles that present the news but don't comment on it

Argumentative Writing

- Editorial and opinion pages in newspapers
- "Elite" magazine articles and commentary
- Most nonfiction books (even those that rely largely on facts tend to be "positioned"; there are very few books that do nothing but present "facts"—almost all will also *interpret* the facts)

THE BLURRY LINE BETWEEN INFORMATION AND OPINION

Below are the headlines and first paragraphs of two articles that appeared the morning after the November 2012 presidential election. The *New York Times* is generally considered "left leaning," or more liberal (aligned with Democrats), so I've placed its excerpt on the left. The *Wall Street Journal* is generally considered "right leaning," or more conservative (aligned with Republicans), so I placed its excerpt on the right. Keep in mind that both of these articles appeared on the front pages of their respective newspapers; both are factual accounts of the election results, but each offers different facts. More importantly, the tone of each is quite different.

The Left: *New York Times*

Divided U.S. Gives Obama More Time

Barack Hussein Obama was re-elected president of the United States on Tuesday, overcoming powerful economic headwinds, a lock-step resistance to his agenda by Republicans in Congress and an unprecedented torrent of advertising as a divided nation voted to give him more time.

The Right: *Wall Street Journal*

Obama Wins a Second Term

President Barack Obama narrowly won re-election, overcoming public doubts about his performance on the economy—doubts that challenger Mitt Romney appeared well-positioned to exploit.

ANALYSIS

The headline: Note that the *Times* focuses on the idea of the country being divided. Also, the idea of Obama receiving "more time" suggests that he hasn't had enough time to correct the country's problems. By contrast, the *Journal*'s headline is absolutely factual. It strikes me that the headline writer might have been thinking of that old grandmother saying, "If you can't say anything nice, don't say anything at all."

Narrowly: The *Times* says only that Obama was re-elected, whereas the *Journal* describes him as having won "narrowly." Interesting choice, one that depends on how you define a "narrow" victory.

Overcoming: It's quite a coincidence that both papers use the word *overcoming*, and because they use it so differently, it's the most revealing word here. In the case of the *Times*, the writers make it sound as if Obama had a lot to overcome, and that at least one key element of this was the "lock-step resistance" of Republicans in Congress. The writer is implying that Republicans unfairly opposed Obama's attempts to improve the economy, but Obama was able to prevail anyway. It makes Obama sound almost heroic, as if he had to battle an unfair opponent but still won. The *Journal*, on the other hand, highlights the "public doubts about his performance." This wording gives significant weight to these doubts and implies that they are reasonable. The fact that the word *doubts* is repeated adds to this impression.

Final thought: Be alert to the fact that what looks like mere information often has opinion embedded in it.

TYPES OF WRITERS

WHO ARE YOU READING?

You'll have an advantage in understanding what you read if you know more about some different types of writers—and what their differences mean for you as a reader.

For example, let's say you read this sentence in an online news site:

> Eating cereal for breakfast is far healthier than eating nothing.

Fine, you think—that sounds reasonable. Your first instinct is to believe the statement. But who wrote it?

The author's name (I'm making this all up to illustrate a point) is Jason Yost. You've never heard of him.

Now, how would you feel about that piece of "information" if Jason Yost were

a. a researcher in nutrition science at Yale University
b. a stay-at-home dad who dropped out of college because his girlfriend got pregnant when they were 22
c. the president of a company that owns five major cereal manufacturers

The answer makes a huge difference in how we interpret the information. This is primarily because of two factors: motivation and qualification.

Motivation

Both the Yale researcher and the stay-at-home dad might be motivated by the search for truth; both might desire to advance our understanding of nutrition.

But the company president is most likely motivated by the desire to sell more cereal. Whatever "the truth" might be, the company president is far more likely to manipulate it so that it serves his needs.

Qualification

Like many things in life, this is not an "either-or" question. Think of it instead as being on a continuum, like this:

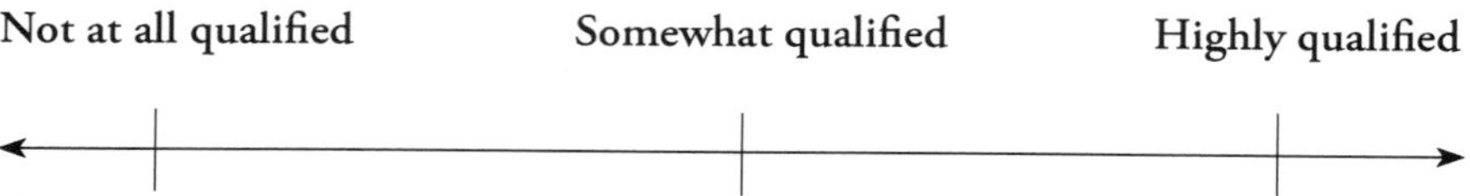

In our example, the Yale researcher is highly qualified, the stay-at-home dad is probably not at all qualified, and the company president—who knows? You'd have to find out about his credentials.

Sometimes it's not so simple to determine what kind of writer you're reading, so first I'll describe some of the basic types of writers you're likely to encounter. In case it's not confusing enough, keep in mind that not all writers fit neatly into these categories. For example, a writer might be a scholar when she publishes papers and books about marine biology—but when she publishes an opinion piece in the *New York Times*, she's both a scholar and an opinion writer.

REPORTERS / JOURNALISTS

Reporters typically work for newspapers and magazines. Generally, they are not specialists in any particular field—rather, they know how to gather information (usually via interviews) and put it together in a way that can be understood by a broad audience. It's also true, though, that at the best newspapers, most reporters are extremely knowledgeable about more specific areas: Congress, the automotive industry, education, etc.

OPINION WRITERS

This category includes people who write editorials, columns, and other opinion pieces. Their work can be found in newspapers, magazines and online publications (like *Slate*, *Salon*, and many others). Often—particularly in newspapers—these writers were once reporters.

When you read opinion writers, it's important to distinguish between those who are "generalists" and those who are "experts." Most opinion writers are generalists—meaning that they typically write about a range of issues, none of which they are "expert" in. For example, a newspaper columnist might write an essay about global warming—and it might be quite well researched and persuasive—even though he or she never did formal academic work in environmental science, geology, or meteorology.

Sometimes, opinion writers *are* experts. Look for a biographical note about the author that explains who the person is; often this will state where the person works, which should reveal a lot. For example, a recent biographical note in the *New York Times* says: "John Farmer, a former attorney general of New Jersey and senior counsel to the 9/11 commission, teaches at Rutgers Law School." The writer, clearly, is an expert on law, which is the subject of his commentary. It doesn't mean he's right, of course—but it does mean that he should know matters of law that a generalist might not.

SCHOLARS

Scholars have been educated (usually through the PhD level) in a specific field, such as sociology, philosophy, English, physics, and so on. Furthermore, most PhD-level work is highly specialized, with the result that the scholar is focused largely on a particular part of his or her field. Within English, for example, that might mean eighteenth-century Russian poetry or post-war American fiction.

When you read a scholar writing in his or her field, you should expect to encounter a high level of language and perhaps some jargon specific to the field. There will likely be numerous references to other research done in the field, as well as footnotes and/or endnotes and a bibliography.

PROFESSIONAL WRITERS

That word *professional* might not be the best choice—but I want it to convey that the writer is an employee, typically of a large company or institution. Unlike a reporter, the professional writer's goal is not (necessarily) to tell the truth; instead, it's to depict the company or organization in the most flattering light. This doesn't necessarily mean that the writer is going to lie to you. But it's frequently the case that these writers stretch, twist, and manipulate facts so that the reader will be sympathetic to the company or organization.

Sometimes you'll find these writers in reputable publications such as the *New York Times* and other newspapers and magazines, many of which will include a biographical note such as, "John Smith is Chief Information Officer for Blandwood College," or "John Smith is the director of security for Giant Computer Systems."

When you see something like that, you should read the author with the understanding that John Smith's first allegiance is not to you, the reader, or to "the truth," but to the organization that pays his salary. When in doubt, do a quick Google search for the author to find out where he works.

CREATIVE WRITERS

These include poets, novelists, short story writers, and some essayists. Many have extensive formal education, while some have little. But we don't look to creative writers for "information"; rather, we read them in order to deepen our understanding of "the human condition."

TYPES OF PUBLICATIONS

Now that you know something about the basic types of writers you're likely to encounter, you should know something about the various publications you might find them in:

- The Internet (I'm leaving this broad purposefully)
- Online news sites
- "Popular" (or general-interest) magazines
- Daily newspapers (including online versions)
- "Elite" magazines
- Scholarly journals

THE INTERNET

You know, of course, what the Internet is, but you should be aware of the great range of materials to be found there. In short, start to think about how you determine which sites are trustworthy and reliable—because many of them aren't. See Chapter 7: Internet Research for more information.

ONLINE NEWS SITES

Again, there's a wide range here, and you should pay attention to who's responsible for the material you're reading. For example, if you find a news story on msn.com, it most likely comes from AP (the Associated Press, generally a trustworthy source of information). But often when you click on a link, you're taken to a "story" that is produced by a smaller, less reliable organization. Occasionally you'll be taken to an advertisement rather than an actual news story.

Basic advice: If the link takes you to a story by AP, Reuters, or a major daily newspaper, it's probably reliable.

"POPULAR" AND/OR GENERAL INTEREST MAGAZINES

What I call popular, or general-interest, magazines are those that have large circulations and are read by a wide range of people. Like newspapers, most of the writing in these magazines is done by reporters. But you will also find plenty of opinion writing—so you'll need to be able to tell the two apart

If you're considering using popular magazines such as *Time*, *Newsweek* and *U.S. News & World Report* as sources for a paper, be aware that they are not highly respected in the academic world. As background information to help you understand the basics of a topic that is unfamiliar to you, these magazines are fine. But if you're looking for depth of analysis, you won't find it here.

DAILY NEWSPAPERS (INCLUDING ONLINE VERSIONS)

Newspapers have played an important role in our country's history, and in democracy in general. (The United States has the strongest protections for freedom of speech—and the press—in the world.)

In recent years, other forms of "journalism," like blogging, have become powerful too, but there are good reasons to look to newspapers—both for information and for argument.

When you read a newspaper (whether on paper or online), you must know if what you're reading is news or opinion. To do so, it helps to know the differences among the three major "parts" of a daily newspaper: news, editorial, and advertising.

News	Includes articles about recent events, trends, or people. (These should not contain opinions, but many media critics say that even "factual" articles tend to show the reporter's bias.)
Editorial	Includes editorials, opinion essays, and columns, usually about timely issues.
Advertising	Sells ads to individuals and companies. (This is how newspapers make money—which they've had a hard time doing over the last 10 or 15 years.)

Typically, those three departments remain totally separate from each other—because you wouldn't want, for example, the advertising department to be able to say to the news department, "Don't run that story on contaminated beef; we have $100,000 worth of beef advertising this month."

Something to think about . . .

The highest goals of journalism have traditionally been accuracy and objectivity. (Objectivity means that you're not influenced by your own biases.) Then some philosopher decided that "objectivity" was impossible, that no matter how objective we may strive to be, we will always be influenced by our biases, our particular intellectual and emotional history. The philosopher was probably right, but this idea has caused people—in my opinion, at least—to become unreasonably suspicious of journalists.

Yes, we detected clear differences in the *Times* and *Journal* coverage of the election earlier in the chapter, and this would seem to be proof that some journalists twist the news to fit their political agenda.

Still, I'd like to believe that most reporters simply try to report the news as factually and clearly as possible. In other words, with objectivity as their goal. Just because it's philosophically impossible doesn't mean that reporters don't still strive for it. And ultimately, it's our job as readers to be

TIP **Read analytically.** When you're reading a book or magazine and you're about to turn the page, guess what the word or phrase on the next page will be. After you turn the page, compare what you predicted to what the writer actually wrote. What's different, and why? On the next page, for example, what do you think the next words will be after "it's our job as readers to be . . ."?

alert to the ways in which writers try to shape (some would say *manipulate*) our understanding of the world.

"ELITE" MAGAZINES

"Elite" is a category I made up because I think these sources differ in important ways from the popular magazines.

First, though, the similarities; like popular magazines, the elites

- can be found (generally) in mainstream bookstores
- are for-profit, with their main source of revenue from advertising
- are published weekly, bi-weekly, or monthly

Now, the differences are important, and they have to do mainly with the way the elites cover the news and issues of the day.

The elites

- print longer articles that go into far more depth
- cover issues that are more complex and less focused on entertainment
- use language that is more sophisticated

Here are some of the magazines that I would include in this group:

The New Yorker	*The New York Times Magazine**
The Atlantic	*The Economist*
Harper's Magazine	*The Nation*

While these publications do not have the same standing as scholarly journals, they are widely respected.

* Yes, the *New York Times Magazine* is part of a newspaper, but the articles and essays published in it tend to be more like those in the other elite magazines. It is only published on Sundays.

TIP **Pay attention to the first and last paragraphs.** Most essays will reveal their purpose in the first paragraph or two, and often return to it in the final paragraph. Note: Some essays will begin by telling a story or doing something slightly unconventional, but in these cases the paragraphs that follow will state the purpose more clearly.

SCHOLARLY JOURNALS

No matter what field you're in, you're going to have to read scholarly journals, so you should understand something about why they're so important to the academic world. First, though, here's how they're different from magazines (both popular and elite):

- Almost all are published by a college or university.
- Most do not accept advertising.
- Articles tend to be less timely than those in magazines and newspapers.
- Few include images or photographs.
- All of the writing is done by scholars in the field.
- The audience is other scholars in the field.
- Many of the articles use language and/or jargon specific to the field.

What this means is that journal articles will typically be challenging to read, particularly early in your college experience.

Only one other piece of information is important to know about journals before you start using them, and that is that they fall into two categories, those that are peer-reviewed and those that are not. Peer-reviewed journals are the most trusted and reliable sources available. "Peer-reviewed" means that experts in the field (for example, leading scholars of abnormal psychology for the *Journal of Abnormal Psychology*) read and review all articles before they are published. These reviewers tend to be extremely picky about how arguments are constructed, how evidence is presented, and so on. As a result, peer-reviewed journal articles should be absolutely trustworthy.

This is not to say that their content will be absolutely *true*. It only means that they shouldn't contain any blatant errors or misrepresentations of fact.

TIP **Ethos, pathos, and logos:** These are the three ways in which Aristotle claimed that speakers persuade their audience. They apply equally well to writing, and you should be aware of how they operate on you as a reader. *Ethos* is an "ethical" appeal to the reader; it means that the writer is presenting herself as trustworthy and believable: "I have a degree from Yale, and my research has been published in many scholarly journals, so you should trust me." *Pathos* is an emotional appeal, one that is meant to evoke feelings of sympathy from the reader: "The chimpanzee had a look of fear and panic in his eyes before the test began." *Logos* is a rational, logical appeal, one that depends on reason: "If scientists are prevented from conducting tests on animals, research into traumatic brain injuries will end."

WARNING: MIND GAMES AHEAD

Passive Voice

Mistakes were made.

~ Presidents Reagan, Bush (senior), Clinton, Bush (younger)

Passive is the opposite of active. Grammatically, this means that the writer switches the subject and the object in a sentence, which forces the verb to change:

Active: The boy hit the ball.

Passive: The ball was hit by the boy.

In active voice, the "true" subject (the boy) of the sentence is first, and it performs the action. This is the most common way of forming sentences in the English language. When you switch it to passive voice, the meaning is exactly the same, at least in this example. But it's a less natural way for us to read the information. That's the main reason to avoid passive voice as a writer. (Note: I'm not saying you should never use passive voice—only that you should know that you're doing it, and do it for a good reason.)

Sometimes, writers use passive voice because it allows them to omit the "true" subject, the person or thing doing the action, as is the case in the quote above: "Mistakes were made." This statement has become famous—and something of a joke among people who follow politics and/or language—because it has been used by all of our recent presidents to avoid taking responsibility. It should make us ask, *By whom* were mistakes made? But often we don't.

In short, passive voice is not just a grammatical issue—it's also an *ethical* one; here's an example that's closer to your world:

Passive: Tuition and fees at the college were raised.

Active: The college's Board of Trustees raised tuition and fees.

In the passive voice, the sentence omits an important piece of information: *who* is responsible for the increase in tuition and fees. As a result, we don't know whom to blame—or maybe it never even occurs to us to wonder who's responsible for this. We simply accept it.

Pay attention to how politicians and businesses use language (particularly when they are doing something *to* us), and you'll see that they love the passive voice because it allows them to imply that things simply happen, and that no one has caused them to happen.

EVASIVE LANGUAGE: THE ETHICS OF COMMUNICATION

In the example below, you can certainly figure out what's being said. But it takes some effort. The companies that write this "legalese" are counting on you being lazy—they don't want to make it easy for you to understand how to cancel your cable service.

A cable TV company

Original	Refunds/Credits will be given only when request for cancellation of service is received by Charter within 45 days of installation of service (30 days subscribing to the service, plus 15 day grace period for formal requests of refund/credit). Only 30 days of service will be refunded or credited.
Translation	We will only give you a refund or credit if you cancel your Charter service within 45 days of installation (30 days after you subscribed, plus a 15 day grace period). We will only refund or credit 30 days of service.

These examples are clumsy and misleading in their original form mainly due to the use of nominalizations—words that could have been verbs but are turned into nouns. Above, the first words (purchase and refunds/credits) are nominalizations. Academic writers and lawyers seem to love nominalizations too, but this appears to be changing—many editors and legal experts are now demanding clearer, more direct language. See end of Chapter 5 for a more thorough explanation.

The lesson

Be alert to the complex ways in which writers try to manipulate you. It will help you become a better student—and a better citizen.

chapter 3

WRITING AS PROCESS

The work will teach you how to do it.

~ Estonian Proverb

Experienced writers know that "writing" is never as simple as typing up some ideas, turning them into sentences and paragraphs, and then running spell-check.

This chapter offers some advice about the writing process, but it's worth remembering that good writers rarely follow these steps exactly as I outline them. Instead, they tend to write in a way that has been described as *recursive*—meaning, roughly, that they go both forward and backward. They might go from brainstorming to drafting and back to brainstorming. Then, they might choose to revise a small portion of their writing so that it says exactly what they want it to, then go back to drafting again.

THE MYTH OF EASY WRITING Every day we read the work of professional writers in newspapers, magazines, and books. Because we only see the finished product—the thing that has been revised and edited (often numerous times)—we might think that the writer simply sat down and typed it. I can assure you that this is almost never the case. Even the most gifted writers have to revise. In most cases, the finished product that we read has little in common with the writer's first draft. Certainly, writing comes more naturally to some people than others. But even for those people, writing is rarely easy, and it almost never comes without effort.

Here's the basic process, in the order I'll discuss it in this chapter:

1. Find your topic
2. Narrow your topic
3. Brainstorm / prewrite
4. Create a thesis
5. Write an outline
6. Write a draft
7. Revise
8. Proofread

Note: I'm assuming that you've already done some reading and research to prepare for the writing.

FIND YOUR TOPIC

All of your college writing begins with some kind of assignment. Do yourself a favor and pay close attention to it. Make sure you know what's expected of you, and reread the assignment occasionally when you're in the process of writing the paper.

If your topic has been assigned to you, skip to brainstorming / prewriting.

Three Suggestions

- Think about which class sessions you found most interesting. Go back and look at your notes for controversial issues, important commentators on the subject, etc.
- Freewrite about the broad subject—write down anything that comes to mind, including your own memories, observations, personal experiences. The goal at this stage is merely to find a possible direction for your research, one that, ideally, you care about personally.
- Explore the subject in books, articles, or online (see Chapter 7 for guidelines). Don't think of this as research yet; instead, think of it simply as a way of exploring the subject in order to find a workable topic. But do keep track of sources you find in case you want to come back to them later when you do have a topic.

NARROW YOUR TOPIC

Start with a basic principle: If people have written entire books about your topic, it's not narrow enough. Instead of writing about technology and education, for example, narrow it down to how technology is changing higher education—or, more narrowly still, how PowerPoint is overused in college classrooms.

One of my students recently began with the idea to write about veterans' issues and higher education. To help him narrow that topic, I asked him to talk about some of those issues. He mentioned a number of concerns, but the one that he seemed most interested in was the G.I. Bill (a government program that pays college expenses for those who served in the military a certain number of years). Even that was a bit too broad, so he eventually focused on the current overhaul of the bill, often called G.I. Bill 2.0, taking the position that the proposed revisions to the bill were unfair to veterans.

Some of the ideas for brainstorming on the next couple of pages can also help you narrow your topic.

BRAINSTORM / PREWRITE

The key to brainstorming is to learn how to outsmart your brain. (See "Your Brain as Obstacle" on page 23 for more on why this is necessary.) Two techniques—freewriting and clustering—are often helpful when you're trying to generate ideas or find direction for your writing.

CLUSTERING

This technique is good for people who are visual. It can be done on a piece of paper (the larger the better), but it is often most successful when done on a big board with many people contributing.

As with other forms of brainstorming, the key is to not limit the flow of ideas. Still, there's a little more critical thinking involved in clustering because it does depend on making logical connections among ideas.

Here's how it works. Start with any idea or topic—try to express it in a single word, or two words at most. For this example, I'll use *education*. (See next page.) Next, think of ways to divide that subject into many parts, aspects, or issues—maybe ask yourself some of the reporter's questions later in the chapter.

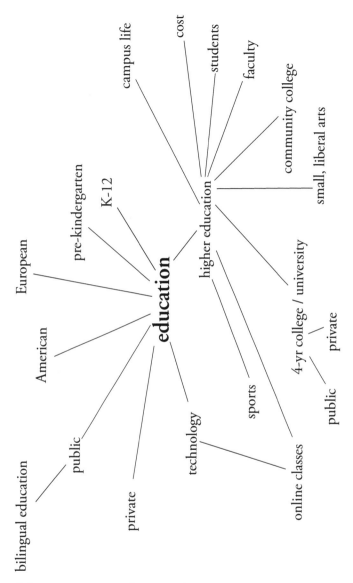

A couple of things to notice: If your web starts to move in one direction (as mine does toward higher education issues), you might start over with "higher education" in the middle and begin branching out again. Also, think about how pieces of this web could be connected. Combining technology, cost, and online classes, for example, could lead to a good topic about how these issues are changing college life.

FREEWRITING

One of the simplest ways to generate ideas for a paper is freewriting. The basic idea of freewriting is this: Write (or type—whichever you can do faster and most easily) quickly and without worrying about whether your ideas are good or whether they make sense. Don't worry about grammar. This isn't writing that you'll turn in—it's just a way to help you figure out what you're interested in, narrow your topic, and discover some possible questions about your topic.

What to do when you're freewriting

- Ask questions about your topic
- Try to connect different parts of the topic that interest you
- Answer some of the reporter's questions on the next page

What *not* to do when you're freewriting

- Worry about grammar or spelling
- Edit yourself
- Delete anything

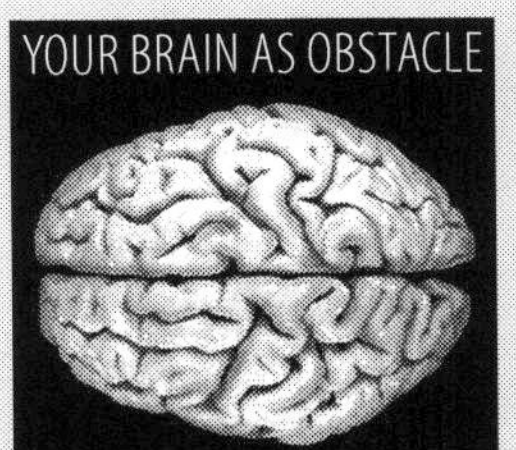

Your brain has many parts, and understanding how they contribute to the writing process—and how they can get in the way—might help you. I'm no expert on the brain, but I do understand three of its most important functions: it stores memories and other information, it processes emotions, and it reasons.

All of these functions are useful, of course, but not all are equally useful at every stage of the writing process. For example, the part of your brain that is capable of reasoning is essential as you move through the middle and later stages of writing—but you don't necessarily want too much of this kind of brain activity in the early stages of writing. Why? Because that's where the Critic lives. He (or she) is inside your brain, where he remembers your past experiences of writing and stops your thought process to tell you that your writing is no good, your ideas are worthless, etc. (When the Critic is active, she is using all parts of your brain—especially the memories and emotions of past negative experiences with writing.)

Enough psychotherapy. The point is simply to keep in mind that we all have self-critical instincts, even the most (seemingly) well-adjusted people. Those instincts are not productive for you in the early stages of writing, so you should do everything you can to keep them in check.

Final thoughts on brainstorming

You'd be surprised how often something useful can come out of what seems like a bad idea. Some of the best ideas come after initially thinking, *That can't possibly work.*

Think about how creative many kids are—they invent games and "pretend" worlds all the time. Why? Because their imaginations are not limited by some "higher" voice telling them that their games are useless or poorly constructed. They just adapt the games, refine them, discard them, and so on. But they keep inventing.

Invention comes largely from a sense of play and often from lucky accidents. If you follow the rules all the time, the imaginative and inventive parts of your brain will never get a chance to function. And even though writing a paper for a class is not typically thought of as a creative act, there is still invention and creativity in the form of the kinds of connections (synthesis) you make.

REPORTER'S QUESTIONS The reporter's five "W" questions (there's also an "H") can help you break a big topic down into smaller parts. These questions can also help you make connections among the parts. Here's an example of applying the reporter's questions to the topic of education:

Who	Students, professors, administrators, parents, school boards, legislators
What	Private vs. public, pre-Kindergarten, grade school, high school, higher education
When	Different time periods, such as 18th century, early 20th century, 1970s, etc.
Where	Rural versus urban or suburban schools, American versus European or other geographic regions
Why	Origins of education: Why did education become "formalized"? Why do we have compulsory education? Why is a college degree so important to employers, or is this changing?
How	Methods of educating people: whole languge versus phonics for debates about how students learn to read, or lecture versus "student-centered" instruction in college courses

CREATE A THESIS

Once you have some direction for your paper, you should start working on a thesis. (This isn't always true—in some cases, it makes more sense to begin with questions and uncertainties and allow yourself to discover the thesis later.)

Topic vs. thesis

Your topic is what the paper is about; your thesis is what you have to say *about* the topic. It's your position, your stance.

Think of it this way—readers can't disagree with you about your topic, but some readers should be able to disagree with you about your thesis. In this chapter, I'll also describe the thesis as your paper's "big purpose."

Sample topic

> Portable electronic devices (cell phones, laptops, etc.) in college classes

How would a reader disagree with that? I can't say, "That topic doesn't exist." (I could, but I'd be wrong; when you think of "the reader," you have to imagine a sane, rational person.) I could say, "But portable electronice devices haven't had any effect on college classes"—but again, I'd be wrong, or at least somewhat irrational.

Sample thesis

> The presence of portable electronic devices in college classrooms has changed the way students and professors interact.

Not many people would argue with this, of course, but an argument against this assertion is possible. Therefore, it's an acceptable thesis statement. If your professor wants a more argumentative paper, your thesis could look like this:

> The presence of portable electronic devices in college classrooms has adversely affected the way students and professors interact.

A good thesis statement should

- take a position
- open up a discussion or continue a "conversation"
- be specific

For example, let's say that you're in an anthropology class that's examining the many languages around the world that are in decline—experts say that of the roughly 6700 languages used throughout the world, half are in danger of "extinction," and one "dies" approximately every two weeks. You would not want a thesis that attempts to take on this very sizable topic. Instead, perhaps, examine a specific language that is considered "endangered." Let's take Irish (or Gaelic, as it's also known) as an example. A more specific thesis statement might investigate whether funding for Irish language television programming is (or is not) merely slowing the inevitable death of the language. That would be sufficiently narrow and specific, and it would also continue a discussion that linguists, Irish people, government officials, and educators have had about the state of the language and what might or should be done to preserve it.

WORK FROM AN OUTLINE (OR NOT)

Some writers like to have a complete outline that breaks down every single element of the paper, and others feel far too constrained by such a plan. At some point in the writing process, though, it's generally smart to write at least a basic, informal outline.

AN INFORMAL OUTLINE

An outline doesn't have to be formal. It can be as simple as this:

1. Introduction, with thesis statement
2. Major point #1
3. Major point #2
4. Major point #3
5. Conclusion

That's the dreaded five-paragraph structure, which many teachers of writing despise. They say that it's too simplistic and limiting. I would argue, though, that many great pieces of writing use some version of this structure, and that most argumentative writing moves through at least two major points that prove the thesis. Also, the simplicity of the structure does not necessarily have to limit the complexity of your argument or the intelligence of your thinking.

The important lesson here is that your paper must have an introduction, a "body," and a conclusion. In the body of the paper, you must have separate distinct "parts"—these parts are generally paragraphs in shorter papers, but they may be sections in longer papers. In books, the "parts" are chapters and sections within chapters.

A FORMAL OUTLINE

If you're one of those hyper-organized people who has to have every last detail planned, this is for you. (Or maybe you should avoid it—because it might do you good to approach writing in a different way.)

A formal outline uses Roman numerals and letters. One of the most basic rules is that if you have a 1 (or an A), you must have a 2 (or a B).

I. Introduction—background: how education has changed in response to technology
   Thesis: Although many people are critical of online learning, it can be beneficial for all involved. (This is an acceptable "starter" thesis but would need to be refined in the actual paper.)

II. Advantages for the college
   A. Uses no classroom space
   B. Reduces maintanence costs
   C. Requires no additional parking lots

III. Advantages for faculty
   A. More efficient
   B. Convenient

IV. Advantages for students
   A. Convenient
      1. Better for busy students
         a. Some are parents
         b. Many work
      2. Easy for those with disabilities
   B. Less intimidating

V. Conclusion

The subpoints (#1 and #2) give evidence for the larger point ("Convenient").

These points explain and/or illustrate the subpoint ("Better for busy students").

Note: I've only expanded part of the Section IV.

"I" STATEMENTS / FIRST PERSON: PROCEED WITH CAUTION

I think / I believe / It is my opinion / The point I am making is

Using the first person in an academic paper is a controversial issue, so I offer here a brief description of the two competing views. Check with your professor for guidance.

Many professors don't allow students to use first person . . . for two reasons: first, they say that students who rely on "I think" (and its variants) tend to make personal claims rather than clearly reasoned points; second, many professors argue that the first person simply isn't necessary, as in this case:

> I believe that George Will's definition of reality television is too narrow, and that he ignores many compelling and worthwhile programs that use the "reality" format.

Simply eliminating the first person results in a more efficient sentence that doesn't lose any clarity:

> George Will's definition of reality television is too narrow, and he ignores many compelling and worthwhile programs that use the "reality" format.

But other professors . . . are encouraging their students to use first person ("I") in some circumstances; they argue that it's good for students to use these constructions as a way of making clear (both for themselves as writers and for readers) what they are saying, and as a way of differentiating this from what their sources are saying. For example, let's say that you've just paraphrased an assertion from one of your sources:

> George Will characterizes the emergence of reality television as the end of Western civilization.

Now, let's say that you disagree with this, and you're going to say so in your next sentence. Using an "I" statement can alert your reader that he needs to shift gears and be ready to encounter your view:

> **I would argue,** however, that Will's definition of reality television is too narrow, and that he ignores many compelling and worthwhile programs that use the "reality" format.

(The transitional word *however* also helps the reader make the shift.)

WRITE A DRAFT

Many writers dislike the sight of a blank page. It can be intimidating, slightly overwhelming. If you have some prewriting and an outline, you have a real advantage. Either way, though, I suggest that you consider starting your draft not with the introduction, but with one of your body paragraphs. Many writers take this approach, with the reasoning that they can't really know how to introduce what they haven't yet written. The point is that there are no rules for drafting; you should jump around the parts of the paper as much as you want. Once you have all the parts in draft form, then you can worry about how they fit together.

Topic sentences

Like outlines, topic sentences often get no respect. They are viewed as overly simplistic, too obvious. Why should you say what the paragraph is going to be about in the first sentence so plainly? Shouldn't you just let the reader figure it out? No, you shouldn't. And there's nothing simplistic about a well-crafted topic sentence, one that lets the reader know what direction your new paragraph is headed in. Furthermore, even the most accomplished and respected writers use them, as in this example (a single paragraph, taken from the middle of a long article):

> But, as private colleges became more selective, public colleges became more accommodating. Proportionally, the growth in higher education since 1945 has been overwhelmingly in the public sector. In 1950, there were about 1.14 million students in public colleges and universities and about the same number in private ones. Today, public colleges enroll almost fifteen million students, private colleges fewer than six million.
>
> – Louis Menand, "Live and Learn," *The New Yorker*

The first sentence signals a clear purpose for that paragraph; everything that follows explains, clarifies, supports, and gives examples for the larger idea stated in the topic sentence. Notice also how the final sentence performs a "concluding" function for the paragraph as well.

Good topic sentences make it much easier for your reader to follow your thinking, but they also have an important function for you as the writer: they help ensure that *you* know what you're doing in every single paragraph of your essay. Writing a clear topic sentence forces you to decide what you're trying to accomplish in a given paragraph, and it might also help you eliminate (or move elsewhere) material that doesn't fit with the topic sentence.

REVISE

First drafts are rarely very good. They are a starting point, little more. If you're lucky, you won't have to start over, but you shouldn't rule that out.

What I'm trying to persuade you to do here—for your own benefit—is change your attitude toward revision. If you see revision as the heart of the writing process (which it is, I and a thousand other writers promise you), you might be more willing to do the sometimes difficult work that is ahead of you.

After you finish a draft, you should at least be able to answer two questions:

- What is the big purpose of the paper? (State it in one sentence.)
- What does each body paragraph do to help support or develop the big purpose? (State each paragraph's purpose in a brief phrase.)

If you can do those things, it's probably time to let someone else read your paper—then ask that person the same questions. By the way, I'm using the phrase *big purpose* in these questions as a different way of saying thesis.

> **MYTH: REVISION IS EASY**
>
> Revision does not mean to "fix" your draft. It's more than simply finding the errors and correcting them. The word itself, *revise*, has its roots in the idea of sight, and suggests "seeing again." Implied in this is the idea of seeing your work in a new way. First and foremost, you want to rethink your ideas—how they connect, how you express them, and what, in the larger sense, they are saying about your topic.

If you or your reader can't answer those two key questions relatively easily, you have two options:

Option #1: Start over. It sounds awful, but it's often a more efficient use of your time. Sometimes, trying to fix a paper that has major problems (especially problems of purpose and clarity) takes more time than simply starting over. Professional writers do it all the time.

Option #2: Find what *does* work in your draft and start with this material; get rid of everything else.

Here's a simple but important concept my students often miss: If you're not sure what your paper is saying, or why it includes any particular piece of information or evidence, then your reader likely won't know either.

Revision through conversation

Another strategy for revision is to imagine your paper as an actual conversation. If you were sitting around with a friend, just talking about this subject, what would both of you be saying? Here's how that conversation might go:

> **You:** I think that students should not be allowed to use laptops or cell phones during college classes.
>
> **Friend:** Hmm.... That's interesting. What makes you think that?
>
> **You:** Well, for one thing, some professors say that students aren't paying attention to what's going on in class.
>
> **Friend:** Isn't that the student's problem?
>
> **You:** Well, yes, but if we want well-educated students, maybe the college policies should help ensure that students are getting the most out of their classes. (This might be a paragraph in your essay that explores the responsibility of the college to create policies that attempt to optimize learning.)
>
> **Friend:** But students have always been distracted—they doodle or stare out the window. What's the difference between that and a laptop, which is just like a different kind of window to stare out of? (Your friend is acting as a *naysayer* here, bringing up a reasonable objection to your assertion.)
>
> **You:** The difference is that an open laptop is also distracting to other students who can see it. (This might be a new point in your paper, perhaps its own paragraph.)
>
> **Friend:** Sure, but a blanket policy prohibiting laptops unfairly penalizes students who simply want to take notes more efficiently.
>
> **You:** That's true, but some recent research suggests that taking notes the old-fashioned way, with pen and paper, can result in better retention.
>
> And so on....

If you can imagine a friend who's difficult to persuade, this will help you come up with objections to your arguments.

ANTICIPATE THE OPPOSITION It might seem like a bad idea to introduce an idea that could contradict your argument, but it can actually make your position stronger. In fact, if you don't deal with obvious objections to your views, your readers often think of those objections, and then they find your argument less persuasive because they believe you can't answer those questions.

PROOFREAD

If you don't proofread your paper, it will most likely contain at least a couple of careless errors. For me, and for many other professors, a paper that seems as if it is the product of a lazy or careless writer is easy to give a low grade to.

Proofreading is actually pretty easy—you're not concerned with the big ideas at this stage, just the correctness of words and sentences. You want the paper to feel polished and professional, so check for spelling errors, missing words, quotation marks turned the wrong direction, anything that might communicate sloppiness to your reader.

I have two specific suggestions that should help you find both careless errors and awkward sentences:

- Read your paper backwards, one sentence at a time (don't read each word backwards—that would be ridiculous). This forces you to focus on each sentence individually and can help you see your writing with fresh eyes.

- Read your paper out loud, or, even better, have someone read it out loud to you. Listen for places where the person has difficulty reading a sentence or finding the right rhythm—that's often a sign that a sentence needs to be rewritten.

TIP: USE THE CLOUD

Don't lose that file—save it to the cloud

I have computers at home and at work, and I also have a laptop. In the past, I had to be careful about working on a document—like this book—from one computer, then making sure I had saved that version (to a thumb drive) and moved it to my other computers. Now, though, thanks to the cloud, I can work on a file at home, give it a moment to sync (a green bird at the top of my screen tells me everything is up to date), and then find the updated version of that file on my two other computers. Amazing, and very convenient.

I can also access all my files from any computer with Internet access.

Both of the sites I recommend here are well established and strike me as very secure. Still, you should take normal precautions with any personal information you store in the cloud.

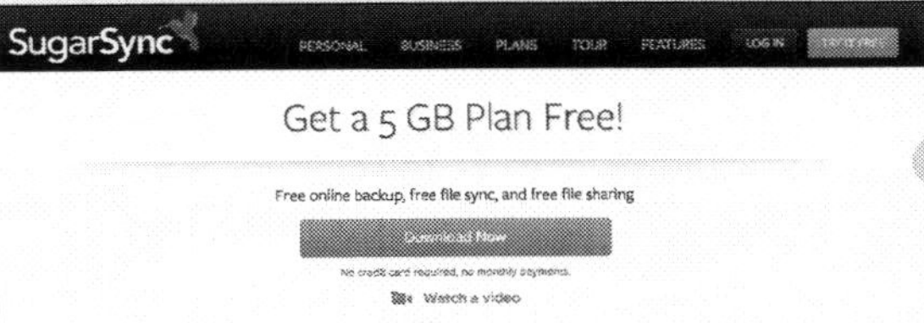

I use SugarSync for all of my personal files. I find it easier to use than Dropbox—though you do have to search to find their free plan: Google *sugarsync 5GB free*.

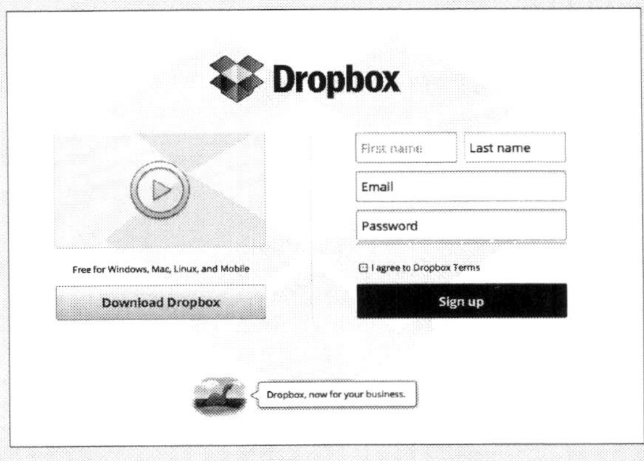

SAMPLE STUDENT PAPER

This paper was written by a student in my English composition course last year. I chose it because it has quality research, strong writing, and solid organization.

How to format your paper

Margins: 1 inch on all sides. Indent all paragraphs 1/2 inch. Use the Tab key rather than typing spaces.

Spacing: Double-space all text. (Under *Format* menu, select *Paragraph* and then *Line Spacing*.)

Specific formatting elements

1 Your last name and page number should appear on every page. See pages 36-37 for how to do it using a header.

2 Your name and class information should appear in the order shown here. Double-space this information just as you do the rest of the paper.

3 Title: Don't use bold, italics or underlining. Also, you generally don't use quotation marks, with one exception: if you use a quotation within your title, that part would need quotation marks. For example, if Kyle had wanted to use part of the quote from the bottom of page 4 in his title, it would look like this:

"Stand Behind a Register and Smile":

The Millennial Generation and Changes in the Workplace

Note: I think Kyle's title is better.

The Colon Is Key: A Brief Primer on the Art of Creating Strong Titles

The title of this box, like the title of Kyle's paper, exemplifies one of the basic guidelines for creating a good title—use a colon. There's a simple formula for the titles of many academic papers: start with something interesting and slightly mysterious, then follow it with a more conventional phrase that clarifies what your paper is actually doing.

Something Creative and Intriguing:

Something Standard that Makes Clear What Your Paper Will Investigate

1 Wright 1

Kyle Wright 2

Professor Cooksey

English 101.29

6 December 2012

New Collar Workforce:

Catalysts for Progressive Change in the Workplace 3

As the Millennial generation, a cohort with dates of birth ranging from the 1980s to early 2000, enters the workforce, analysis surrounding this new generation attempts to uncover just what this digitally native, feedback-driven demographic has to offer. As this demographic begins to gain distinction from its predecessor Generation X, these young people will have a significant impact on the modern workplace. Many generational analysts insist that Millennials lack disciplinary traits needed in the workplace. Professionalism, structure, and management skills are common shortcomings of this demographic, according to a survey conducted by Adecco, a human resources consulting firm (Bednarz). Of course, it's true that many of the characteristics of Millennials clash with the traditional work environment; however, the Millennial generation will ultimately transform this outdated workplace into one that fosters efficiency, productivity, and flexibility. Replacing expectations of conventional structure and adherence to process, this modern take on the workplace is one that promotes and properly utilizes this generation of assertive and refined workers—a generation of born entrepreneurs.

Numbering in at around sixty million and representing ten to fifteen percent of the workplace, Millennials are poised to be powerful

Paper continues on page 38.

TIP: WORD PROCESSING

Creating a Header with Page Number

Many students have trouble with page numbers and headers. MLA formatting requires that you put your last name and a page number on every page; here's how to do it.

1. Start by clicking on the **Insert** tab.

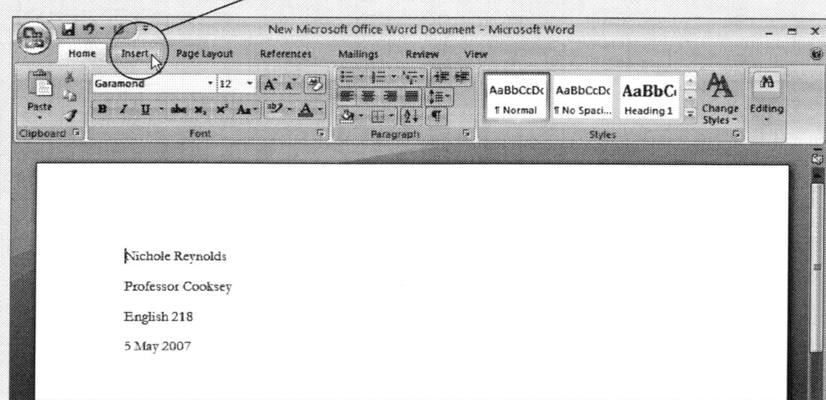

2. Now click on the **Header** icon.

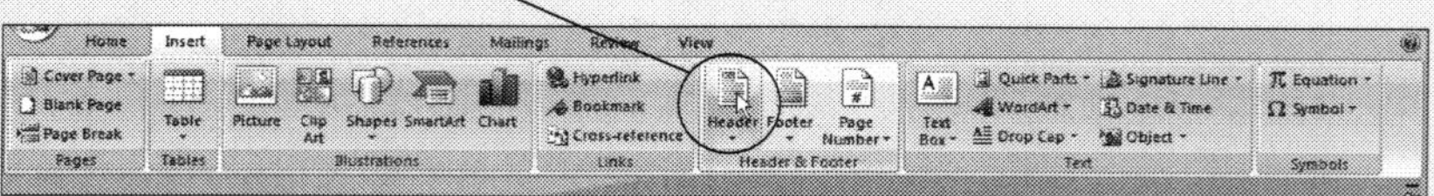

3. Now click on **Page Number**, which will reveal more options. Choose **Insert Page Number**.

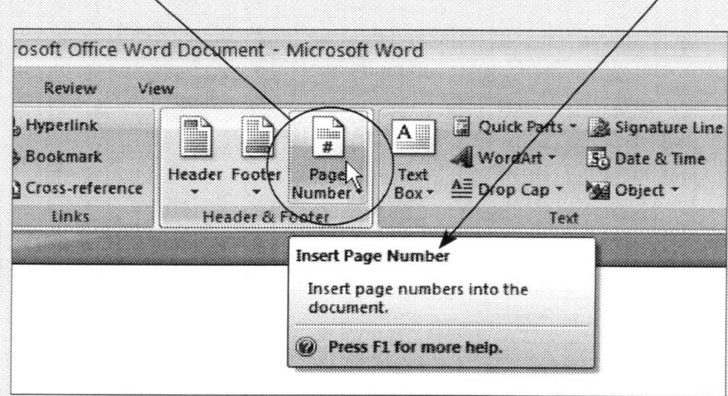

TIP: WORD PROCESSING

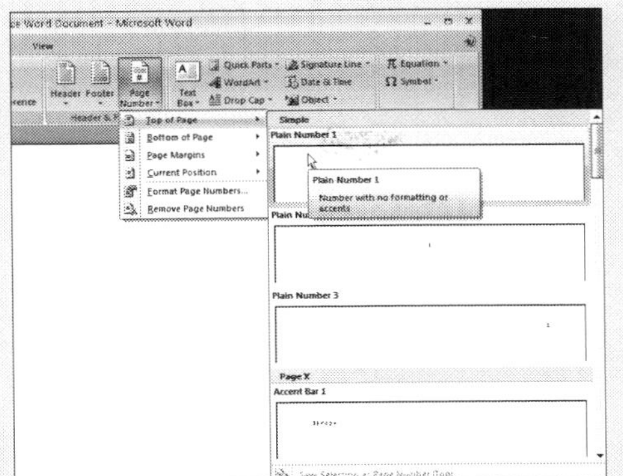

3. Choose **Top of Page** and then **Plain Number 1.**

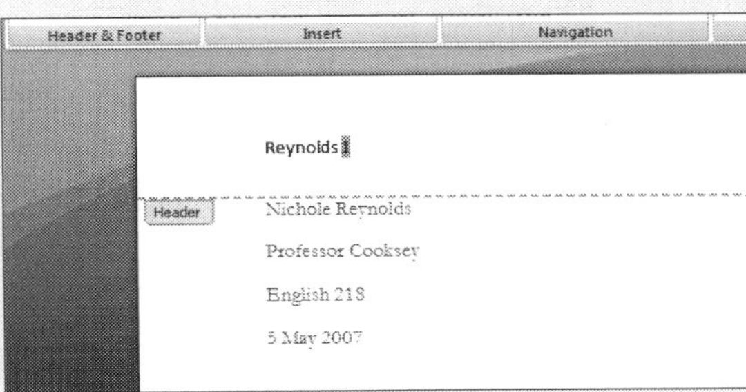

4. Now you're in the header; type your last name and a space before the number.

5. Switch to the **Home** tab.

6. In the **Paragraph** control, choose **Align Text Right.**

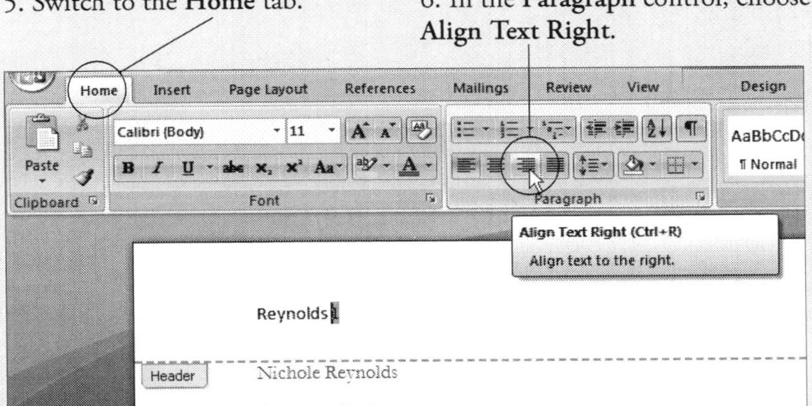

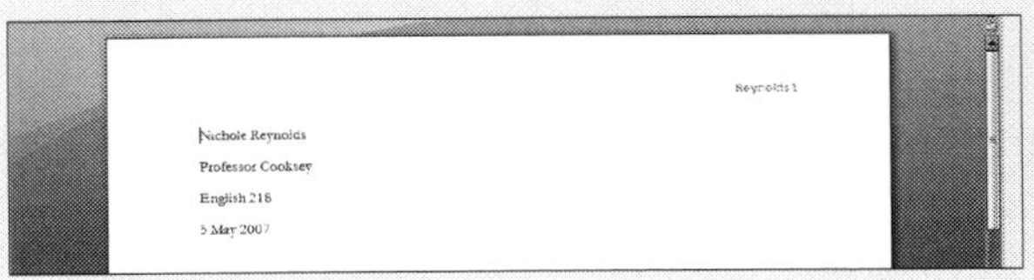

This is how it should look when you're finished. Simply click somewhere in your text to get out of the header.

Wright 2

drivers of the economy, both as employees and as consumers (Bannon). Employers must work to meet the needs of Millennials entering the workplace, including flexibility, compensation, and opportunity. In turn, the characteristics of the Millennial generation will come to meet the needs of the business, redefining the workplace and creating a symbiotic relationship between employee and employer that will promote efficiency, results, and balance for both sides of the working relationship.

Stretching Our Legs: A Focus on Flexibility 4

In a recent study conducted by MTV, 79 percent of Millennials thought that they should be allowed to wear jeans to work, compared to only 60 percent of Baby Boomers (Kiisel). While dressing for comfort rather than professionalism may be an insignificant fashion change, it may indicate a much larger trend of freedom and flexibility in the workplace. Dan Schawbel, a Gen Y career expert and the founder of Millennial Branding, argues that this change toward a flexible and often casual work environment is caused by the Millennial generation's desire for a deeper work-life integration. Unlike previous generations, Millennials don't talk about balancing work and life, but rather about blending them.

Work-life balance is a growing concern for the Millennial generation, who refuse to work long hours at the expense of their personal life. According to the Pew Research Center, when asked to rate how important various life goals were to them, Millennials ranked being a good parent

4 Kyle uses section headings in this paper, which can help the reader see the organization of your paper more clearly—but they are no substitute for good transitions. Also, some profesors may not want you to use section headings, so check first.

Wright 3

as a top priority, and the importance of the family outranked fame and fortune (Bannon). Life goals such as parenting and spending time with the family may cause Millennials to challenge the conventional nine-to-five workday in favor of a flexible schedule that allows for better integration of their personal and professional lives (Bannon). To create a balance between a productive career and a healthy lifestyle, the Millennial generation's redefined workplace emphasizes quality of work over number of hours and success over a structured adherence to schedule.

A few companies—Best Buy, I.B.M., and Capital One Financial Corporation—have begun to embrace the Millennial desire for a healthy and flexible work-life balance in radical and exciting ways. Best Buy human resource managers Cali Ressler and Jody Thompson have developed the Results-Only Work Environment, or ROWE. This program offers employees complete control over their time, so long as their work gets done. As Ressler and Thompson explain in their book *Why Work Sucks and How to Fix It*, "A true ROWE has unlimited paid vacation time, no schedules, no mandatory meetings, and no judgments from co-workers and bosses about how employees spend their days" (61). Instead of rewarding employees on how many hours they log or how well they navigate office politics, ROWE advocates say that a relentless focus on results forces managers to be clear about expectations, allows employees to create a work life balance that is right for them, and increases productivity while reducing cost and employee turnover rates. 5

5 Note the uses of dashes to set off information that might have been confusing if Kyle had used commas, primarily because the three companies named here need commas between them. For more on dashes, see Chapter 5: Editing.

Wright 4

6 Even at Best Buy headquarters, however, ROWE isn't universally accepted. Tyler Shaw, a Best Buy employee and participant in the ROWE program, acknowledges, "There are some people who feel hostile about ROWE and want to continue micromanaging" (qtd. in Alsop 171). Managers voice concerns about this radical movement, perceiving it as an attempt by employees to get away with getting paid for "slacking off" (Barr). Telecommuting and working remotely have been around for years, but little evidence is available to show that these changes do much more than improve employee satisfaction and eliminate commutes (Weber). Shaw encourages his colleagues to look at ROWE from an economic perspective: "People spend their time like money, and time has power because it is a limited, nonrenewable resource. People spend their time in the most efficient manner possible to get the desired outcome." Through the implementation of a Results Only Work Environment, companies have boosted both economic results and employee morale. After migrating to a ROWE, departments at Best Buy reported productivity increases of 35 percent (Blakely). In addition, Best Buy's Strategic Sourcing and Procurement Team boosted employee retention by 27 percent, and saw a 50 percent increase in cost reductions over two years.

The Ambitious Generation

Raised in a world surrounded by breakthrough advancements—the boom of the internet, social media networks, and mobile computing—the

6 Note the excellent transition Kyle has created here. It works well because the first few words pick up on the ideas from the previous paragraph, but the word *however* lets you know that he's shifting into a different direction.

Wright 5

Millennial generation has become synonymous with ambition, a trait that defines a born entrepreneur. This ambition, and the many ways it benefits the symbiotic relationship between the business and the Millennial, is a dominant factor driving change in the redefined workplace.

7 While many Millennials are not driven to succeed by a fancy title or the corner office (Salzberg), this generation is interested in how their contribution to the workplace will make a positive difference. As John Spano, a human resources director for a movie theatre company, observes, "If you expect them to stand behind a register and smile, they're not going to do that unless you tell them why that's important and then recognize 8
them for it" (qtd. in Twenge 217). Regardless of position or rank in the company hierarchy, Millennials' ambition will drive them to make suggestions to improve the work environment. Although this may seem disrespectful of authority, businesses should recognize these suggestions as contributions to the symbiotic relationship between employer and employee; managers should reciprocate by offering reasonable opportunity to pursue these ambitions "not by wearing a colorful T-shirt on a special project once a year, but [through] their actual work" (Salzberg). If managers properly utilize the ambition of this generation they can unleash the potential of "all that mobility and access to information" (Salzberg), and can build a diverse, networked, and transparent work environment.

7 This sentence uses information from a source (Salzberg) in the first half of the sentence, but then offers a view that is clearly Kyle's in the second half of the sentence.

8 Kyle's source (Jean Twenge) was quoting her own source, John Spano; Kyle handles this complex documentation perfectly using the parenthetical reference and the "quoted in" construction to show where *he* read the information. See Chapter 10 for more information.

Wright 6

9 Some argue, however, that the ambition of the Millennial generation does not always bring positive change to the workplace. As sociologist and Millennial critic Jean Twenge observes, "The optimism of youth, combined with the instant gratification that technology has provided, often leads to impatience" (219). Some young people will enter the workplace with unrealistic expectations of promotions, or see their career development process as a zigzagging line that allows them to jump around the company hierarchy at their leisure. "This is especially true of the most qualified young people," explains Twenge, "they have been encouraged to have lofty ideas about their future" (219). In this situation, both parties must be reasonable about basic expectations in the workplace. While a company may provide flexibility in terms of time management, "employees control the throttle on how hard they work" (Alsop). If aiming for senior management positions, Millennials should be aware that they are going to have to work hard, often putting in long hours and travel. On the other hand, recruiters promising flexibility may mislead Millennials into believing they can work where and when they want from day one of an entry-level position, when in reality these flexible options may only be available to a small group of experienced employees.

Looking Forward

In the coming years, due to the retirement of baby boomers and the relatively smaller size of Generation X, corporations will find Millennials

9 Kyle provides a clear **topic sentence** for this paragraph; this sentence plainly states what Kyle will be doing now: exploring some complications to the argument he has been making. We call these competing voices **naysayers.** Using language like "Some argue" is an excellent way to force yourself to recognize competing perspectives.

Wright 7

to be in high demand in the job market. As the workplace changes, companies will need to consider how they "attract, retain, and leverage the future of our workforce" (Bannon). Employers looking to unlock the potential of a generation of born entrepreneurs must work to embrace Millennial characteristics and utilize generational talents and skills. By creating a flexible work-life balance and harnessing the ambition that motivates this generation, businesses and Millennials can foster the symbiotic relationship that brings a fresh look and new energy to the working environment, while encouraging this generation of emerging leaders to continue driving positive change in the workplace.

10

10 Kyle's conclusion wraps up the paper nicely. Notice that he only uses one source here, which is appropriate—you want to make sure that *yours* is the dominant voice in the conclusion. The concluding sentences reveal his voice and his view on the subject, but these are not merely a restatement of the introduction; instead, he looks slightly beyond the scope of the current thinking on the subject to offer predictions about the future of Millennials in the workplace.

Note: Double space *all* lines.

Your last name & page number

Works Cited

Adams, Susan. "Older Workers, There's Hope: Study Finds Employers Like You Better Than Millennials." *Forbes*. Forbes Magazine, 24 Sept. 2012. Web. 4 Dec. 2012.

Alsop, Ronald. *The Trophy Kids Grow Up: How the Millennial Generation Is Shaking Up the Workplace*. San Francisco: Jossey-Bass, 2008. Print.

Bannon, Shele, Kelly Ford, and Linda Meltzer. "Understanding Millennials in the Workplace." *The CPA Journal* 81.11 (2011): 61. *Academic OneFile*. Web. 24 Nov. 2012.

Barr, Corbert. "Why Doesn't Everyone Work in a Results-Only Work Environment (ROWE)?" *Think Traffic*. Insanely Useful Media, 31 May 2009. Web. 4 Dec. 2012.

Bednarz, Ann. "Hiring Preferences Favor Mature Workers over Millennials: Study." *Network World*. Network World, Inc., 9 Oct. 2012. Web. 4 Dec. 2012.

Blakely, Lindsay. "What Is a Results-Only Work Environment?" *CBS News*. CBS Interactive Inc., 25 Sept. 2008. Web. 4 Dec. 2012.

Conning, Denise, and Devika Cook. "Bridging the Generational Divide in the PACU." *The Dissector: Journal of the Perioperative Nurses College of the New Zealand Nurses Organization* 40.1 (2012): 27-36. *Academic OneFile*. Web. 24 Nov. 2012.

Harris, Peter. "How Job Hopping Can Be Good for Your Career (And for Your Employers)." *Workopolis*. N.p., 27 Mar. 2012. Web. 4 Dec. 2012.

Wright 9

Holtzclaw, Eric V. "Hiring Millennials? Here's What You Need to Know." *Inc.com*. Mansueto Ventures LLC., 24 Sept. 2012. Web. 4 Dec. 2012.

Kiisel, Ty. "Gimme, Gimme, Gimme—Millennials in the Workplace." *Forbes*. Forbes Magazine, 16 May 2012. Web. 5 Dec. 2012.

Miller, Matt. "Why You Should Be Hiring Millennials." *Forbes*. Forbes Magazine, 3 July 2012. Web. 4 Dec. 2012.

Ressler, Cali, and Jody Thompson. *Why Work Sucks and How to Fix It: The Results-Only Revolution*. New York: Portfolio/Penguin, 2011. *Google Books*. Web. 2 Dec. 2012.

Salzberg, Barry. "What Millennials Want Most: A Career That Actually Matters." *Forbes*. Forbes Magazine, 3 July 2012. Web. 4 Dec. 2012.

Stillman, Jessica. "Millennials Are Born Entrepreneurs. Wait, Really?" *Inc.com*. Mansueto Ventures LLC., 6 Dec. 2011. Web. 4 Dec. 2012.

Twenge, Jean M. *Generation Me: Why Today's Young Americans Are More Confident, Assertive, Entitled—and More Miserable Than Ever Before*. New York: Free Press, 2006. Print.

Weber, Jonathan. "Why Telecommuting Doesn't Work." *Management 101*. NBC News, 6 Sept. 2009. Web. 2 Apr. 2013.

Please see Chapter 10 for in-depth coverage of MLA documentation.

A WRITER TALKS ABOUT WRITING

CANDACE CLEMENT

Writer, Activist, Musician

Photo by Seth Jackson

Candace was my student at HCC for two years, and she was also the editor of the campus newspaper (I was the faculty adviser). We eventually became friends, and now, almost seven years after she left HCC, I still see her often. She was always a very good writer, but she struggled with it more when she transferred to Smith College to major in American studies. She graduated cum laude five years ago, and this interview was done during her final year at Smith.

Candace now works full-time for Free Press, a non-profit organization devoted to media reform. She also sings and plays guitar in my favorite local band, Bunny's A Swine.

Tell me about how you start writing a paper.

I don't know what the thesis is going to be so I have to read about it [the subject] before I can figure that out. And then I have to start writing before I know what I think about it. I feel like I make a jump from reading to writing, and that's when I'm really thinking. I'm thinking as I'm writing. 'Cause I write, like, crazy shit. I swear, I write half sentences. I'll write furiously for ten minutes about something, and then it'll just stop. I'll run out of steam. And maybe four or five sentences out of that actually end up in the paper, but I'm like, oh, okay, that's what I think of this.

I'm really bad at writing first drafts. The first draft is very stream-of-consciousness. I don't hesitate, I don't block anything.

You're not writing for an audience then. It's just for yourself.

Exactly. And sometimes, if I'm struggling with that, I'll try to write it to someone I know, like a friend of mine. "So, Tessa." She's my best friend. "This is what I'm thinking about this." And it'll help me because sometimes it gets too abstract in that stream-of-consciousness state. The first draft really is that stream-of-consciousness craziness, swearing, throwing in whatever, not finishing sentences. In the second draft I'll try to take that and write it to someone else, like Tessa.

Do you ever actually send it to her? In e-mail or something?

No, I've never done that. It's not always her, but I try to make it more verbal. So I'm not worrying about word choice and verb placement. I'll write the word *like*, I'll write the word *whatever*. I'll write *and stuff*. Because it just helps move the stream of thought or whatever along.

For the first few years of college, I would never do drafts of any sort. I wouldn't think I was doing drafts. But I was. I would write something, hit save, walk away and come back later. Now, there's more of a draft that happens, because I'll print something when I hit a dead end and I'll cut it up and I'll start rearranging it. Maybe I'll even split paragraphs. I'm big on short paragraphs when I'm in that process. If there's a cohesive thought that needs its own separate thing, it's in its own paragraph. And then I'll later join them and fuse them as necessary.

I'll play with the order of it. Then I write the transitions in and out of each paragraph. Unless there are two paragraphs that really need to go in a linear fashion, I'll save the first and last sentence of each paragraph to write much later in the process.

Sounds smart.

I think that's one of the things that when people say, *This is good writing*, they mean that it transitions well. I'm not totally great at it. In fact, sometimes because I wait so long in the process, that suffers. Another thing—and this is kind of a side-note, but something I would really advocate for. It's the downside of waiting till the last minute. You *need* to walk away for several hours, if not 24 hours at a time. Not look at it, not think about it, and then read it again. And I'm really bad about doing that. The one thing you'll catch is stupid grammatical errors.

That's also why it's good to have another person read it, too. Which I'm also very bad at doing. I'm insecure about my argument. I'm not really insecure about my style. But my argument—by the time it's developed, I'm more protective of it, and I don't want to share that with anyone but the professor. But I miss so many stupid mistakes as a result of that.

You know, a week after I hand in a paper, I almost always go look at it again, and say, *I can't believe I handed this in, and I can't believe I got whatever grade I got.* Except for one professor [a notoriously tough grader at Smith], who wrote on one of my papers, "I look forward to you knowing more about history." Well [with hurt look on face], I look forward to that too, I guess.

chapter 4

COMMON ERRORS

This is just the sort of nonsense up with which I will not put.
~Winston Churchill

Winston Churchill, England's prime minister during World War II, was famous for his wit and his eloquence. I doubt he ever made many "mistakes" in language, but his concern for what grammarians call "correctness" didn't stop him from making fun of the sometimes absurd rules that grammarians create. In the quote above, he's cleverly ridiculing one of those slightly absurd rules, namely not to end a sentence with a preposition (*up*, in this case). Grammatical rules are intended to enhance clarity, but Churchill's sentence illustrates that blindly adhering to (some) grammatical rules can produce comical and ridiculous sentences.

Correctness is a complicated subject, one that we English teachers don't always agree on. And the rules change over time as people refuse to conform to them; a hundred or so years ago, for example, this was considered correct: "He forgat his book."

A more contemporary example: people have started to use the word *anxious* to mean *excited*, as in, *I am anxious to see the new restaurant*. But the word's traditional meaning has to do with worry and anxiety, not excited anticipation: *I am anxious about my test results*. Still, many people are unaware of the "real" meaning of the word and use it to convey excitement. Can we really say it's wrong if so many people use it that way? Eventually, the dictionary will most likely offer both definitions, to reflect how people are actually using the word.

In short, the "rules" are always in flux. But that doesn't change the fact that you should learn and follow them in your writing, particularly in academic and professional situations.

COMMONLY CONFUSED WORDS

4.1 accept / except

Please **accept** my gift of $14,000 so you can buy a car.

Any car is fine, **except** a purple one.

4.2 all right (not alright)

Even though you see it all the time, there is no such word as *alright*. It's all wrong, all the time. (Don't feel bad if you didn't know this—I was on my way to earning a second master's degree before I learned it.)

The man left the emergency room when he decided he felt **all right**.

Note: You should also know that *all right* is informal—you probably shouldn't use it in academic writing.

4.3 a lot (not alot)

A lot of people went to see the artist's video of David Beckham sleeping.

Alot is not correct—don't use it. Also, you should know that while it is correct, *a lot* is informal; in academic writing, it would be better to express a large number more precisely: More than 2,000 visitors saw the artist's video in the exhibition's first week.

4.4 a part / apart

He is **a part** of the oldest club on campus.

This usage, as two words, means that he *belongs* to the club.

Apart from her car insurance, she paid all her bills without her parents' help.

This usage, as one word, means that this one expense is *separate from* the others.

4.5 effect / affect

Effect is (almost always) a noun:

Moving out of his parents' house had at least one positive **effect**: It forced him to get a job.

Affect is (almost always) a verb:

Moving out of his parents' house negatively **affected** his bank statement.

A complication you will only rarely encounter: Effect can also be a verb. In that case, it means *to bring about, or to cause to occur.*

The Board of Education hopes to **effect** change on a system-wide basis.

An additional complication you will encounter even less often: *Affect* can also be a noun, meaning emotional state; the pronunciation is different too, with the stress on the first syllable.

The referee's pleasant **affect** prevented the players from yelling at him, even when he made a bad call.

4.6 imply / infer

Speakers and writers *imply* things:

The speaker **implied** that college freshmen were irresponsible.

Listeners and readers *infer*—or come to a conclusion about something—based on what they hear and read.

We **inferred** from the speaker's comments that he believed college freshmen to be irresponsible.

4.7 it's / its never: *its'*

It's is a contraction (the apostrophe shows that a letter has been "contracted," or taken away) and always means one of two things: *It is* or *It has.*

It's been raining all day. (It has been raining all day.)

It's going to be a long day. (It is going to be a long day.)

Its is always possessive:

> The dog wagged its tail.

(If you wrote **it's** by accident, the sentence would say: The dog wagged it is tail.) See pages 67–69 for possession rules.

4.8 lose / loose

Lose is a verb; *loose* is an adjective:

> If you keep playing like that, you're going to **lose** the game.
>
> When the bolts came **loose**, the wheel spun off the axle.

4.9 then / than

Then shows when something happened:

> We ate breakfast, and **then** we went hiking.

Than makes a comparison:

> Stewie's argument was more persuasive **than** Brian's.

4.10 there / their / they're

There shows location:

> He put the clothes over **there.**

Their shows possession ("ownership"):

> That is **their** house.

They're is a contraction of *they are*:

> **They're** not going to be home.

4.11 to / too

To is a preposition and an "infinitive":

> I'm going **to** the game. He's planning **to** quit.

Too is an "intensifier":

> He has **too** much rice. I was **too** tired to go.

4.12 who / which / that

Don't use *that* when you refer to people.

> **NO** Those are the students **that** wrote the editorial.
>
> **YES** Those are the students **who** wrote the editorial.

You can use *that* when you refer to inanimate objects:

> Here are the papers **that** need to be revised.

Note: you can also use *which*, but most American grammarians recommend *that*. In the next sentence, however, which is the only correct choice:

> The revised papers, **which** I've attached to this e-mail, are ready for your comments.

A simple guideline: If you have a construction like this and you're trying to decide between *that* and *which*, use *that* if there's no comma, and *which* if there is. See also pages 70–71 or do a Google search for restrictive versus nonrestrictive clauses.)

4.13 Who's / whose

Who's is a contraction of **Who is.**

> **Who's** the man with the crooked hat?

Whose is possessive; it shows that something belongs to someone or something.

> That's the man **whose** hat is crooked.

4.14 would have / would've never: *would of*

Writers make this mistake for a good reason—because they write what they hear, or what they say.

> His argument **would have** been more persuasive if he had included better evidence.

Note: In formal writing, it's best to avoid contractions. If the writing is informal, it might be acceptable to write **would've**.

4.15 you and I vs. you and me (and other related errors)

Whenever you hear "That's between she and I," the speaker has made a grammatical mistake, and it's one that you should learn how to avoid in your writing.

Grammar people call it an example of "hyper-correction," meaning that the person who says something like "between she and I" believes he's being extra conscientious, grammatically speaking. He remembers being corrected by English teachers when he said things like, "Me and Josh are going to the movie." The teacher would have said, sternly, "You mean, *Josh and I* are going to the movie." And the teacher would be right because *Josh and I* are a subject (they're doing something), not an object (having something done to them, or receiving an action). So if you said, "The teacher hates me and Josh," you'd be correct, because in that case *me and Josh* are objects—they are receiving the teacher's hatred (or what they imagine to be her hatred; she was probably just trying to help).

Let's look at some examples.

subject object

> Sally loves Hank.

When you introduce another person being loved, that's when things get complicated—both in love and grammar. I should say, it gets complicated when the other person is a pronoun: **I / me** instead of Fred, **she / her** instead of Wanda, etc.

> Sally loves Hank and **(I or me?)**.

The trick is to mentally remove *Hank and*; then it's easy to see the right choice. Think of it this way: You'd never be tempted to say, *Sally loves I*, right? So why would you be tempted to say, *Sally loves Hank and I*?

YES Sally loves Hank and **me.**

Now let's change Hank to a pronoun too. Is it *he* or *him*? Same principle: You wouldn't say, *Sally loves he*. You'd say, *Sally loves him*. So:

YES Sally loves both him and me.

Believe it or not, that's correct. It should *not* be, *Sally loves both he and I*. Never ever ever. No matter how many times you hear people on TV say it—it's not right, and educated people know the difference.

Note: If you're bothered by how your sentence sounds when you write it correctly, consider changing things around. Instead of saying, Tom sent an invitation to Betsy and me (*not* Betsy and I), you could reverse the order: *When Betsy and I received Tom's invitation, we hoped we would be out of town that weekend.*

THE IMPORTANCE OF SOUND

Sound does matter in language, both in writing and speaking; when the grammatically correct way of writing something results in a sentence that sounds wrong, try to rewrite it. Often this means changing a sequence of two or three sentences, rather than just a word or two.

When you use a preposition (*between* in this example), the same rules apply:

NO That is between he and I.

YES That is between him and me.

4.16 your / you're

Your shows possession:

Your hat is crooked. **Your** beliefs are ridiculous.

The second example is abstract. See Abstract Possession later in this chapter.

You're is a contraction of you are:

If you don't leave now, **you're** going to be late.

COMMON SENTENCE ERRORS

Think of writing as being like a house. You, the writer, are like the architect who designs the house. (You're also the general contractor, the electrician, the painter, etc., but we'll keep the analogy simple for now.) When it comes to grammar, though, you're more like an engineer than an architect.

Engineers are the ones who decide if a house is going to work, structurally. When the architect designs a balcony that hangs thirty feet over the back wall of the house, it's the engineer who would say, "That's not going to work." The engineer is less concerned with how the house is going to look, and much more concerned with whether or not the it's going to stand up and keep everyone inside dry.

That's how you need to think about sentences.

We're not talking about what would look interesting. We're talking about whether or not the thing "works" grammatically—because if you have a paper full of flawed sentences, it's like a house where the walls are in the wrong places, or built from the wrong materials. It might look like a house, but it won't be safe. Now apply that analogy to a paper with numerous sentence errors: It might look like a paper, but it won't really make a lot of sense, and it might even fail in its most basic mission—to communicate with a reader.

4.17 Run-on / comma splice

A run-on sentence has more than one complete thought in it; it becomes a run-on when you don't connect—or separate—those thoughts grammatically.

> Jim drove his car into a pile of snow he could not get the car back onto the road.

In that "sentence," there are two complete thoughts; the first one ends after snow. That's a pretty obvious error, and not one that many students would make. But this version of the same mistake is less obvious:

> Jim drove his car into a pile of snow **then** he could not get the car back onto the road.

This sounds better, but it's still a run-on, because **then** doesn't have the grammatical power to connect the two complete thoughts.

Note: A comma splice has essentially the same problem as a run-on, but it has a comma between the two complete thoughts—which still isn't enough to connect the parts:

Jim drove his car into a pile of snow, he could not get the car back onto the road.

Run-ons and comma splices can be corrected in two basic ways—either by separating the complete thoughts (with a period or semicolon), or by connecting them (with a variety of methods).

Separating with a period—acceptable but often simplistic

Jim drove his car into a pile of snow. He could not get the car back onto the road.

Connecting —a better solution

With a coordinating conjunction:

Jim drove his car into a pile of snow, **and** he could not get the car back onto the road.

With a dependent word:

After Jim drove his car into a pile of snow, he could not get the car back onto the road.

Or with a dependent word, reversing the parts (and changing a pronoun):

Jim could not get his car back onto the road **after** he drove it into a pile of snow.

4.18 Fragment

A fragment is an incomplete sentence. It can happen for a variety of reasons, most often because you've made one part of the sentence dependent—without giving it another part that's independent to balance it, like this:

When there is no more gas left and cheaper sources of fuel can't be found.

It's that first word, "when," that makes the sentence a fragment—because it's a dependent word in this case. Like most fragments, the sentence leaves the reader hanging, waiting for something else. The thing you're waiting for is the independent clause, the thing that will make the sentence complete:

When there is no more gas left and cheaper sources of fuel can't be found, more research will be devoted to alternative energies.

Fragments *can* be good

Fragments aren't always a mistake. Experienced writers use them for good effect—they can break up the rhythm of your sentences and provide emphasis, as in this example:

> Storing explicit memories and, equally important, forming connections between them requires strong mental concentration, amplified by repetition or by intense intellectual or emotional engagement. The sharper the attention, the sharper the memory. (193)
>
> ~ Nicholas Carr, *The Shallows: What the Internet Is Doing to Our Brains*

The second sentence is the fragment, of course (there's no verb). But it's effective here because the sentence that precedes it is long and complex. The simplicity of the second sentence provides a quick, accessible way of thinking about the complex information in the previous sentence.

Purposeful fragments can help balance long sentences and provide a quick punch of information. But use them sparingly—too many fragmented sentences (even when written intentionally) will look gimicky, and they will lose the power to grab the reader's attention.

4.19 Subject-verb agreement

Subjects and verbs have to agree "in number":

> **NO** The paper go into that drawer.
>
> **YES** The paper goes into that drawer.

4.20 Compound subject (subject-verb agreement)

When you have a two-part subject joined by *and*, you need a plural verb:

> The chair and the table **are** in the truck.

Some writers are thrown off by the fact that table (which is singular) is right next to the verb, which might make them choose *is* for the verb instead of *are*. But *are* is correct because chair and table, together, become plural.

When you have a two-part subject joined by *or*, you choose the verb based on the subject closest to the verb.

The plumber or his assistant **does** a final inspection of the work.

Plural

The plumber or his assistants **do** a final inspection of the work.

4.21 There is / There are (subject-verb agreement)

When you start a sentence with one of these constructions, you have to choose the right verb (*is* or *are*) based on whether the subject is singular or plural

There *is* one way to get rid of fleas on your dog.

There *are* many ways your dog can get fleas.

In the first sentence, the subject is *way*, which is singular.

In the second sentence, the subject is *ways*, which is plural.

Note: Starting a sentence with *There is* or *There are* is weak—try to rewrite your sentence to avoid this construction. (See Chapter 5: Editing.)

4.22 –ing subject (subject-verb agreement)

When your subject is an –ing word (also called a *gerund*), you need a singular verb. (This error, by the way, appeared in the *New York Times*.)

NO The awarding of contracts to Pearson in Kentucky and Virginia illustrate the problem.

YES The awarding of contracts to Pearson in Kentucky and Virginia illustrates the problem.

4.23 Interruptions (subject-verb agreement)

In English, we tend to like the subject and verb right next to each other, but sometimes we want to separate them, as in this example:

NO The Abominable Snowman, though never found by researchers, live on in myth.

YES The Abominable Snowman, though never found by researchers, lives on in myth.

Some writers might have been tempted to think that the plural noun *researchers* would make the next verb *live* instead of *lives*. But if you remove the "interruption" (all of the information inside the two commas), it's easy to see that *Abominable Snowman* is the subject and that *lives* is the right verb.

4.24 Pronoun reference errors

These errors usually occur when you have a singular (meaning one) subject that you mistakenly connect to a plural (more than one) pronoun.

NO **Each student** must submit **their** financial aid form by Friday at 5 p.m.

Four possible solutions:

YES Each student must submit his or her financial aid form by Friday at 5 p.m.

YES Students must submit their financial aid forms by Friday at 5 p.m

YES You must submit your financial aid form by Friday at 5 p.m.

YES Financial aid forms must be submitted by Friday at 5 p.m.

4.25 Faulty parallelism

Parallelism means that two or more elements are consistent with each other.

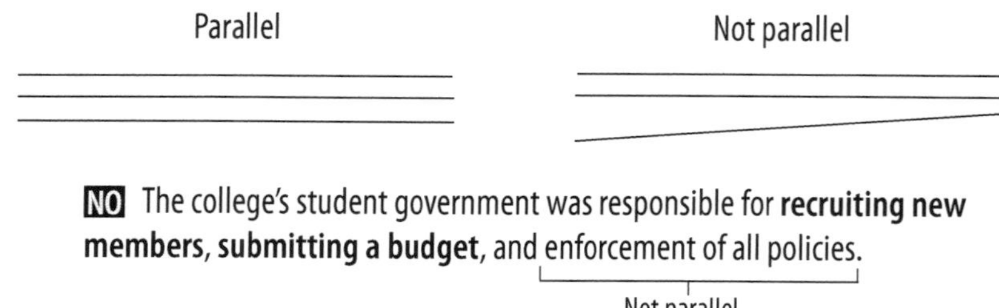

> **NO** The college's student government was responsible for **recruiting new members, submitting a budget**, and enforcement of all policies.
>
> (Not parallel)

The first two responsibilities are parallel to each other, because they both begin with an -ing verb and then follow with a noun. The third responsibility, in order to be parallel, must also start with an -ing verb (enforcing) and follow with a noun.

> **YES** The college's student government was responsible for **recruiting new members, submitting a budget**, and **enforcing all policies**.
>
> (Parallel)

A FEW RULES WORTH LEARNING

I've always believed that English teachers rely too much on rules—and that students learn to write more clearly as a result of reading and practice. Still, you'll avoid a lot of mistakes if you refer to these guidelines for apostrophes, commas, titles, and capitalization.

Apostrophes for contractions

A contraction means that something becomes smaller. With words, contractions are formed with apostrophes, like this:

is not = isn't

The apostrophe here shows that a letter has been removed. The principle is the same even if the apostrophe replaces more letters:

would have = would've

Note: Avoid contractions in formal academic writing.

Apostrophes for possession

When we speak, we create the "sound" of possession by adding an *s* sound. But when we write, we use an apostrophe.

I offer four rules for apostrophes here. If you learn the first two, you'll get the apostrophe right 70 percent of the time. Learn all four and you'll never make an apostrophe mistake.

Rule #1: Don't add apostrophes to words that are simply plurals.

In this example, some people would be tempted to put an apostrophe somewhere in the word *cars*.

Five cars were left in the parking lot overnight.

But nothing "belongs" to the cars here, so there's no apostrophe.

Rule #2: In most cases, just add 's to the word doing the possessing:

Here, the trunk "belongs to"—or is a part of—the car, so you add **'s** to car.

One car's trunk had been broken into.

Here, one cat "possesses" a paw:

The cat's paw got caught in the door.

The rule is the same if the person/animal/thing doing the possessing ends with the letter s; pretend that the cat is named James:

James's paw got caught in the door.

Also, it doesn't matter if the cat had managed to get two paws stuck in the door—the possession rule would be the same:

The cat's paws got caught in the door.

Okay, it probably matters to the cat, but it doesn't matter to us, at least not grammatically.

Rule #3: When more than one person or thing is doing the possessing, the apostrophe usually goes after the s.

In this example, *cars* is plural in the first sentence (so no apostrophe), but possessive in the second sentence (so it needs an apostrophe).

> Five cars were left in the parking lot overnight. All the cars' windshields were smashed.

Also remember that it wouldn't matter if we added an adjective: "the cars' *dirty* windshields."

Rule #4: Possession with plural words like men, women, etc.

The plural form of most words ends with an s: tables, chairs, elephants, houses, trees, and so on. But some words—like *women, people, men*—form a plural without the final s. When the plural form of a word does not end in s, add 's.

> The women's room is down the hall, on your left.

(The room that "belongs to" women is down the hall.)

Commas

Six rules cover just about every use of the comma. Here they are:

After introductory material

> After the judge's recess, the plaintiff disappeared.
>
> Nonetheless, all the cars were ticketed.

Around an "interruption"

> James, the oldest boy in the class, was also the tallest.

With items in a list or series

> The recipe calls for apples, pears, peaches, and cinammon.

(Note: The comma after the next-to-last item in the list—*peaches*, in this case—is the subject of great controversy among grammar geeks. Some consider it optional, while others insist it must be included. If you're curious, google *Oxford comma*.)

Between two complete thoughts, with a conjunction

The police officer arrested the student protesters, but a judge later ruled that the officer had used excessive force.

With many uses of *which* (aka nonrestrictive clauses)

Her favorite food was artichokes, which he found repulsive.

I explain the grammatical rule in the next few examples, but it may be just as helpful for you to simply listen for the slight pause that usually occurs in these constructions.

When to use *that* versus *which* can be confusing, particularly when you're trying to determine whether or not you need a comma; grammatically, the key is to know whether you're dealing with a restrictive or a nonrestrictive clause:

Cell phones that ring during movies are extremely annoying.

Here, the meaning of cell phones is *restricted*—the sentence says that in *one specific circumstance* (during a movie) cell phones are annoying. No comma is needed.

Cell phones, which became widely available in the mid-90s, can be extremely useful.

Here, the meaning is *not* restricted—the sentence says that cell phones can be extremely useful. The other piece of information is not essential to the meaning of the sentence. (Yes, this example is very similar to the "interruption" rule.)

With quotations (see also Chapter 7)

Red Barber once said, "Baseball is dull only to dull minds."

Note: If the quote flows grammatically within the sentence, then the comma is usually omitted:

Red Barber once described baseball as being dull "only to dull minds."

Titles

Generally, titles of shorter works go inside quotation marks; titles of longer works are italicized.

Quotation marks

Article in a newspaper, magazine, or academic journal:

David Carr's "A Guide to Smartphone Manners"

Essay in a book: Philip Lopate's "Portrait of My Body"

Short story: Alice Munro's "Boys and Girls"

Poem: Seamus Heaney's "Digging"

Episode of a TV show: "Put the Dog Out" (episode of *Family Guy*)

Song: Sex Pistols' "Anarchy in the U.K."

Italics

Book: Herman Melville's *Moby-Dick*

Collection of essays, stories, or poems:

Seamus Heaney's *Collected Poems:1965-1975*

Textbook: *Quick and Dirty: A Compact Guide to Writing, Reading, and Research*

Album: Neutral Milk Hotel's *In the Aeroplane Over the Sea*

Movie: *Lost in Translation*

Television show: *Family Guy*

Complication: Sometimes, particularly with poets, fiction writers, and essayists, the name of a book will also be the name of a story, poem, or essay within the book. For example, Seamus Heaney's first collection of poems was called *Death of a Naturalist*. So, when referring to the book

ABSTRACT POSSESSION

Often, the idea of possession is obvious: Something "belongs" to someone: Jim's hat, or Tina's car.

But there's another form of "possession" that is less obvious—mainly because it isn't physical. I call it abstract, or conceptual, possession. For example:

Mike's anger caused him to lose his job.

Does Mike "possess" his anger? Not in any physical sense—but in a grammatical sense, yes.

The most common form of abstract possession is emotional: Mike's anger, Tina's love of her children, Paul's fear of dogs, etc.

But other types of possession are even harder to detect because they involve what I'll call an "abstract state of being."

Mike's inability to control his anger caused him to lose his job.

Again, it's hard to think of "inability" as belonging to Mike, but it does.

as a whole, I would italicize the title. However, there's also a poem by the same name in the book; when I refer to that poem, I would use quotes: "Death of a Naturalist."

The title of *your* paper

Capitalize every word in your title except for the following:

articles: a, an, the

prepositions (even long ones): of, on, to, for, with, about, through (and many others)

conjunctions: and, but, or, so, yet, nor, for

infinitive: to

Example:

An Analysis of Symbiotic Relationships among Birds, Bees, and Flies

Generally, you capitalize all the "important" words.

Also, when you put a title on your own paper, don't do anything to it—no quotation marks, no italics, no bold. Nothing. The only exception to this is if you have a quote within your title, like this:

Landscape, Memory, and Myth in Heaney's "Personal Helicon"

Capitalization

People's names

Ernest Hemingway, Homer J. Simpson (it doesn't matter that he's a cartoon character—it's still his name)

Places

Paris, France; Wheeling, West Virginia; North Carolina's Outer Banks

Complication: Some "places" don't get capitalized: southern Virginia (because there is no place by that name), western Massachusetts

However, you do capitalize regions in some cases (but not compass directions):

He is thinking about going to college in the South.

To get to the bank, you drive south towards Atholl.

Many people died when the West was settled.

Chicopee is west of Worcester.

When the compass direction (north, south, east, west, northeast, southwest, etc.) becomes a "place," you should capitalize it. When it simply tells which direction something is in, you don't.

Languages / people / cuisines

English, French, Chinese, Russian, Portuguese, etc.

Organizations / institutions

Congress, the Department of Labor, Seattle Central Community College, United Auto Workers (because it's the formal name of a union)

Brand names

Kleenex, Apple (the computer), Panasonic, Tide (laundry detergent)

Professional titles / academic titles

Typically, if someone's title comes before his or her name, you capitalize it; if it comes after, you don't:

> I met with Vice President Bausch for almost an hour last week.
>
> The meeting was led by Robert Bausch, a vice president at the college.

Additional resources

To learn more about grammar and other issues of correctness, I recommend the site at Purdue University; do a google search for *owl purdue grammar*.

chapter 5

EDITING

The difference between the right word and the almost right word is the difference between lightning and the lightning bug.

~ Mark Twain

I believe more in the scissors than I do in the pencil.

~ Truman Capote

Editing is the last thing you should do before you turn your paper in. Make sure you leave yourself some time for this step—it can make a big difference in how "polished" your paper feels, and therefore also what kind of grade it gets. Remember, though, that this is not the time to worry about the quality of the "big" ideas—just focus on words and sentences.

EDITING BASICS

- Work from a printed copy of your paper—it's easier to see errors that way.
- Read your paper out loud, slowly.
- Read your paper backwards, one sentence at a time. This is useful because it disrupts your usual flow and forces you to focus on each sentence individually. This is particularly helpful if you have grammatical errors.
- Ask a friend to read it and mark obvious problems. If your friend is a good writer, ask her to make other sentence-level suggestions too.

If you really want to find out whether or not your paper reads well, have a friend read it out loud to you. Listen for places where she has trouble reading a sentence—these can indicate problems with rhythm and emphasis.

You have three jobs when you edit (in order of importance):

- Find and correct obvious errors
- Cut useless words and phrases
- Rewrite sentences to improve clarity, rhythm and readability

FIND AND CORRECT OBVIOUS ERRORS

See Chapter 4 for many common errors that you should be able to correct in editing. Make sure, for example, that you have not misspelled anyone's name; when you refer to Jane Smiley as *Jane Smily*, your professor will doubt your ability to pay close attention to details.

THE DANGERS OF SPELL CHECK Spell Check is useful, of course, but it doesn't replace common sense. For example, if you misspell *definitely* (as many people do), Spell Check will frequently offer *defiantly* as the first option to correct your error. But this is an entirely different word, with a very different meaning. If you blindly accept every suggestion Spell Check makes without thinking about the word, you're likely to end up with some ridiculous mistakes. As always, think for yourself.

CUT USELESS WORDS AND PHRASES

I know, you're trying to get *up* to your professor's minimum length requirement. She said you have to have a five-page paper, and you've just barely got five. And now I'm telling you to cut words. But it's worth it—professors appreciate crisply written prose that doesn't include wasted words. (I should, for example, change the end of that sentence to this: *doesn't waste words*.)

Useless words

Inexperienced writers often use a lot of words and phrases that don't add anything to their sentences. They're filler—get rid of them. (The worst offenders are the first five, in bold.)

really	individual	all things considered
very	specific	in a manner of speaking
basically	type of	as a matter of fact
actually	particular	definitely
kind of	in the process of	as it were
sort of	more or less	
generally	for the most part	

More words that can replace phrases

All of the words below in bold are appropriate for academic writing, whereas the words in the two columns to the right are often used when writers are trying to make their sentences sound more impressive (without actually *saying* anything impressive).

because	for the reason that the reason for due to the fact that in light of the fact that	on account of considering the fact that on the grounds that because of the fact that
when	on the occasion of under circumstances in which	in a situation in which
about	as regards with regard to where ________ is concerned	in reference to concerning the matter of
now / today	at this point in time in this day and age	at the present time
must / should	it is crucial that there is a need/necessity for	it is necessary that it is important that
can	is able to has the capacity for	has the opportunity to has the ability to
may / might	it is possible that it could happen that	there is a chance that the possibility exists for

REWRITE FOR CLARITY AND PRECISION

VAGUE LANGUAGE: IT, THIS, THINGS, ETC.

My colleague Elizabeth Trobaugh strictly limits the use of the word *this* in student papers. Her opposition to the word is well-reasoned: Writers frequently fail to be clear what words like *it, this, things,* and *issues* refer to. Or they have a vague idea but don't take the time to be specific about the reference. Here's a sequence of sentences from a recent student paper:

> So maybe other cultures have **things** we don't. Sometimes they are heavily valued, other times not so much. In **this** case **it** is.

What *things*? In *which* case *what* is? Be specific. As a writer, your job is to make it as easy as possible for the reader to understand what you have to say. (I can't even offer you a revised version of that sentence because I don't know what, exactly, the writer was trying to say.)

Here's an example, from a student essay about obesity in America:

> David Zinczenko grew up with a "daily choice between McDonalds, Taco Bell, and Kentucky Fried Chicken." He believes that **it** isn't the eater's fault. **It**'s the issue that fast food restaurants are everywhere and Americans have no choice, but to eat **it.**
>
> **Revised:**
>
> David Zinczenko grew up with a "daily choice between McDonalds, Taco Bell, and Kentucky Fried Chicken." He believes that **teen obesity** isn't the eater's fault. Because fast food restaurants are everywhere, Americans have no choice but to eat **unhealthy foods.**

THERE IS / THERE ARE

These constructions are a poor way to begin a sentence—they tend to be weak because they allow you to avoid saying anything about your subject. For example:

> There is a reason why good writers avoid empty phrases.

What's the reason? Why not tell us in the same sentence?

> **Revised:**
>
> Good writers avoid empty phrases because readers resent being forced to read unnecessary words.

"TO BE" VERBS

One of my high school teachers made us write an entire paper without using any "to be" verbs. In other words, we couldn't use *am, is, was, were, are, been, being,* or *be*. It's difficult not to use these verb forms because they're the most common verbs in the English language. (In that sentence, I used two: It *is* difficult, and they *are* the most common....)

I wouldn't suggest that you try to eliminate *all* of these verbs in your writing, but it can be helpful to replace as many of them as possible with stonger, more expressive verbs.

Here's an example, using my sentence from above:

> It's difficult not to use these verb forms because . . . .

As I thought about how to get rid of that first *is*, I couldn't just think of a synonym for *is difficult*. I had to think about the entire concept and try to express it differently. Here's what I came up with, and it's no accident that I think the revision is superior:

> We rely on these verb forms because . . . .

Or, if you didn't want to use *We* :

> Writers rely on these verb forms because . . . .

USING DASHES

The dash is a way of separating information. The key difference between the dash and other "separating" marks of punctuation (commas, semi-colons, periods) is that the dash is a stronger interruption, and it generally feels less formal than those other marks.

A word on what a dash is *not*: it's not a hyphen. A hyphen is a punctuation mark that connects two or more words: re-create, ex-wife, door-to-door salesman.

TIP: WORD PROCESSING

Creating a dash. . . It seems simple, but word processing programs don't always do what you want them to. So, allow me to explain:

Type two hyphens immediately after Kevin—don't use the space bar.	Emily walked away from Kevin--
Start typing the next word, again with no spaces after the hyphens. Once you've typed the next word and then hit the space bar, the hyphens will turn into a dash.	Emily walked away from Kevin—and away

Like other marks of punctuation, the dash has grammatical rules that apply to it. These rules depend on whether you use a single dash or a pair, so we'll discuss these separately.

As a single dash

> Emily walked away from the restaurant—and away from an entire way of life.

In this example, the dash allows you to add another piece of information to the sentence. It could have been done with a comma instead of a dash, but the dash provides more emphasis. It gives the second part of the sentence more weight and importance.

A single dash can also allow the part after the dash to function as a definition (not in a dictionary sense) or explanation of what precedes it, like this:

> They made a list of the blockbusters over the decades—the first Tonka trucks, the Frisbee, the Hula-Hoop, the Rubik's Cube.
>
> – Hanna Rosin, "The Touch-Screen Generation," *The Atlantic*, April 2013

In that sentence, what comes after the dash gives some examples of the blockbusters; Rosin could also have used a colon (:) instead of the dash. A comma in place of the dash, though, would have made the sentence confusing because of the three commas that separate the toys. The dash is the perfect choice here.

Here's another example from the same article; in this usage, the dash allows the writer to add some additional information and call attention to it.

> The gathering was organized by Warren Buckleitner, a longtime reviewer of interactive children's media who likes to bring together developers, researchers, and interest groups—and often plenty of kids, some still in diapers.
>
> – Hanna Rosin, "The Touch-Screen Generation," *The Atlantic*, April 2013

There's one other way that a single dash can be used, and it's a bit unusual grammatically in that it allows the writer to connect two complete thoughts:

> Also, they were not really meant to teach you something specific—they existed mostly in the service of having fun.
>
> – Hanna Rosin, "The Touch-Screen Generation," *The Atlantic*, April 2013

In that sentence, the part that comes after the dash is a complete thought, which means that in this case the dash has the same grammatical "power" as a period or semicolon.

A dash always calls some attention to itself, so you should use it sparingly. It's particularly useful when your sentence includes a number of commas; the dash, or paired dashes, can help keep the grammar of your sentence clear.

As a pair of dashes

When you use dashes in a pair, remember that they function almost exactly like parentheses. Grammatically, the principle is identical: Whatever you put inside the dashes can be removed without affecting the grammar of the sentence.

In terms of meaning, too, paired dashes resemble parentheses. What you find inside the dashes is something of an afterthought, an aside, something interesting but not essential to the sentence. What the paired dashes do that parentheses don't is call more attention to the information inside them. Parentheses are like a whispered comment, while dashes are like a poke in the ribs.

> ReD is one of a handful of consultancies that treat everyday life—and everyday consumerism—as a subject worthy of the scrutiny normally reserved for academic social science.
>
> – Graeme Wood, "Anthropology Inc.," *The Atlantic*, March 2013

The information inside the dashes here is an additional piece of information that's not critical to the sentence; however, in placing this brief phrase inside the dashes, the writer has brought more attention to the idea of consumerism.

Here's another example that works in a similar way.

> Still, given the food industry's power to tinker with and market food, we should not dismiss its ability to get unhealthy eaters—slowly, incrementally—to buy better food.
>
> – David H. Freedman, "How Junk Food Can End Obesity," *The Atlantic*, July 2013

And finally, an example of how paired dashes can help you create a lengthy, complex sentence.

> The study adds to a river of evidence suggesting that for the first time in modern history—and in spite of many health-related improvements in our environment, our health care, and our nondietary habits—our health prospects are worsening, mostly because of excess weight.
>
> – David H. Freedman, "How Junk Food Can End Obesity," *The Atlantic*, July 2013

This final sentence would be somewhat demanding for many readers, but I do think it holds together well—and it does so in large part because of its sophisticated use of dashes.

TRANSITIONS

Between paragraphs

You've probably heard that you're supposed to have transitions between paragraphs, but what does that mean exactly? In short, it means that there's a link between the ideas in one paragraph and the ideas in the next.

The example below, from a student paper, shows the final sentence of a paragraph about low wages for Wal-Mart employees, and then the next paragraph, which focuses on the lack of health insurance options for those employees.

> . . . It is the greed of the management of this company that keeps their workers earning below poverty wages.
>
> Many of the employees at Wal-Mart are unable to get an adequate health plan for themselves and their families due to costly health care costs. . . .

The original has no transition between the two paragraphs, but it's pretty easy to create a link between those ideas. The simplest way to do it is to use an idea from the last sentence of the first paragraph, briefly, in the first sentence of the next paragraph.

> . . . It is the greed of the management of this company that keeps their workers earning below poverty wages.
>
> Low wages are only part of the problem, though, because many Wal-Mart employees are unable to get an adequate health plan for themselves and their families due to costly health care costs. . . .

A different version, one that makes a closer connection between the two issues:

> . . . It is the greed of the management of this company that keeps their workers earning below poverty wages.
>
> With such low wages, most Wal-Mart employees are also effectively cut off from adequate health care for themselves and their families. . . .

Between sentences

Many writers assume that transitions are only for paragraphs, but you need them between (and often within) sentences too.

> Wal-Mart's health insurance covers only 50.2 percent of their 1.4 million U.S. employees. The industry average is 65 percent of workers insured.

The key to making a good transition between these two sentences is to think about how the ideas relate to one another. These ideas are in contrast, so you want a transitional word or phrase that shows that contrast:

> Wal-Mart's health insurance covers only 50.2 percent of their 1.4 million U.S. employees **whereas** the industry average is 65 percent.

TRANSITIONAL WORDS / PHRASES

SIMILARITY	EMPHASIS	ADDITIONAL SUPPORT	CONTRAST	CAUSE AND EFFECT	EXAMPLE
likewise	certainly	additionally	but	accordingly	for example
similarly	even	again	however	consequently	for instance
also	indeed	also	in contrast	hence	namely
too	in fact	and	on the other hand	so	specifically
just as	of course	as well	whereas	thus	to illustrate
	truly	equally important	on the contrary	therefore	
		further	nevertheless		
		furthermore	still		
		in addition	yet		
		moreover			

DIRECTNESS: AVOIDING STUPID WRITING

The worst kind of bad writing is that which tries to make itself sound smarter or more complex than it actually is, like this:

> Interest in the possible applicability of TRIZ tools and techniques to the world of management and organizational innovation issues continues to grow.

Some of you may be impressed by that—you may think it's sophisticated and complex. It's complicated, that's for sure. But only in the structure of the sentence, not in content. Using that sentence, I'll show you the four key principles for bad writing.

How to write badly in four simple steps

1. **Remove any human presence**: The sentence is "disembodied," which means that it doesn't have a "body," or person. The first word of the sentence is *interest*, so who's interested? Businesses, I assume, so why not say so? Some writers seem to think that if you remove human beings from sentences, the writing will sound smarter. But all it really does is make the sentence harder to understand.

2. **Turn verbs into nouns (also known as nominalization)**: *Applicability* is a nominalization of the verb *apply*; *innovation* is a nominalization of *innovate.*

3. **Use more words than you need**: *Possible* and *the world of* are not needed in this sentence.

4. **Move the verb as far away from the subject as you can**: The subject is *interest*, and the verb is *continues*; there are eighteen words between the two, which makes it extremely difficult to connect them. Our most basic desire in English sentences is for a subject and a verb, preferably close together.

* * *

The guiding principle of the writing in that TRIZ sentence is this: If it's hard to read, you must have to be smart in order to write it. Good writers know that this principle is wrong; furthermore, following it reveals a contempt for the reader. When political and business owners communicate with you in this way, you should demand to know why they want to make their policies and practices harder rather than easier to understand. Do they have something to hide?

Here's how the TRIZ sentence could be written more clearly, without any loss of meaning:

> Businesses can become more innovative in management and organization when they apply TRIZ tools and techniques.

I'm not absolutely certain I've said what the original writer intended—but that's because his/her writing is unclear. At any rate, I think I'm close. And I've taken a sentence that was twenty-two words and reduced it to fifteen words (32 percent more efficient!); also, it has a real subject (businesses), followed immediately by a verb, and this combination of changes makes the sentence far easier to read.

English is a flexible, adaptable language, but when writers violate the principles that make it work, they create sentences that don't communicate effectively.

FINAL THOUGHTS

Does this scenario sound familiar? You've waited until the day before a paper is due to start working on it. You stay up until three in the morning to finish it, get a few hours sleep, finish the works-cited page, give it a title, and print it. You rush to campus, make it to class just in time, and triumphantly hand in your paper.

Then, when you get the paper back, you see that the professor has marked several mistakes you could've found if you'd left yourself more time. And the grade reflects all those careless mistakes. (In my class, a sloppy paper with more than a couple of careless errors will rarely get a grade above a C.)

Take time to edit and proofread—at least an hour, if not more. Also, the more time you can allow to pass before doing the editing, the better. If you have a little distance from your work, you're more likely to notice problems.

Turning in a polished paper—even one with some flaws in thinking—is almost sure to get you a better grade than one with obvious errors and awkward sentences.

chapter 6

RESEARCH BASICS

Research means that you don't know, but are willing to find out.

~ Charles Kettering

True genius resides in the capacity for evaluation of uncertain, hazardous, and conflicting information.

~ Winston Churchill

WHY DO YOU HAVE TO WRITE RESEARCH PAPERS?

To get a grade

Of course this is why you write papers, but if you're *only* writing for a grade, you're unlikely to do your best work. Writing formal papers is an important part of college for some good reasons, like these. . . .

It makes you smarter

A confession: When I was a college student majoring in philosophy, I never enjoyed writing papers. I loved seeing the connections among ideas, and how one philosopher's thinking extended or transformed someone's else's work, but I often dreaded the writing. I'd done all the important work of learning about a subject, so why did I have to write about it?

I came to understand, slowly, that it was in the writing that I was really learning how to make sense of what I'd read. Don't get me wrong—I love the idea of reading purely for pleasure. But at the heart of higher education is a different way of interacting with ideas. And that kind of interaction *requires* writing. We need to write in order to learn *what* we think, and *how* we think it.

In short, some of our most significant learning takes place when we write.

It improves the world

In Chapter 2, I said that all writing is rhetorical, meaning that at some level it is always trying to persuade the reader to accept the view(s) of the writer.

When a piece of writing is published as an essay or book, it becomes part of what might be called a "larger conversation," and it's in this conversation that writers have the power to improve the world. For example, when Michael Pollan wrote his book *The Omnivore's Dilemma*, about how agriculture works in America, he was simply continuing an ongoing conversation about the relationships among farms, industry, business, the environment, the oil industry, and our dining room tables. Plenty of people disagreed with him—but in that disagreement, too, the conversation continued. Pollan doesn't get the last word in the conversation, but he's now part of it, and as a result, people are talking about these issues in new ways. In a not-so-small way, Pollan has changed the world.

Of course, when you write a paper for a college class, that paper isn't likely to be published and influence how people think about a subject. But if you try to think in those terms, it might help you write more purposeful papers.

EXTENDING THE CONVERSATION

Your reader (that mythical stranger who is interested in your subject matter but doesn't know you—and is not your professor) has two basic expectations about your paper:

1. You have something to say.

This means that your paper is driven by an idea that is at least somewhat new or original. It can't simply say what has been said before—why bother writing it if someone else already has?

2. You are aware of what has already been said.

In order for an intelligent reader to trust you, you must demonstrate that you're familiar with the important work that has been already been done on your subject.

If you think of any particular subject—global warming, the effects of technology on higher education, or how Millennials are changing the workplace—you can easily imagine it as a "conversation." One observer says one thing; another person responds to it, perhaps disagrees. Another commentator comes along and enters the conversation by disagreeing with both of the previous thinkers. And so on. The conversation moves in new directions, considers new evidence, continues to evolve. Sometimes the conversation becomes angry and unpleasant, but it's still a conversation. No one ever has the last word.

It's easy to see how this way of thinking about writing and research has implications beyond the classroom. Only in a country that preserves real intellectual freedom can ideas be debated so freely. By extension, when your professor asks you to write a paper, he or she is asking you to participate in one of the most important forms of democracy available to us: the ability to think freely and share ideas.

INTERACTING WITH SOURCE MATERIAL

When you interact with your sources, you're doing two things—first, announcing to your reader, "Here's what someone else has to say," and second, in effect, saying, "Here's what I have to say about that."

Writing a paper where you only do the first part—reporting what other people have said/written—is generally pointless. (Some professors do assign papers that are merely reports, though, so make sure you know what your professor expects.)

"Here's what someone else has to say."

When you use source material, it's important that you do so responsibly, which means quoting, paraphrasing, or summarizing accurately. Typically, you want to use a *signal phrase* ("According to Michael Pollan…") to introduce the source material; this will make it clear that the idea or information belongs to a source, not to you.

Summarize: to state the main idea of a text (or part of a text) in a shortened form.

> **Note:** Usually a summary is only a fraction of the length of the original; you can summarize a three-page essay in a few sentences, but you can't summarize it in three pages—the summary must be a small fraction of the total. For a longer work, like a 300-page novel, you can summarize it in a few sentences or a few paragraphs, depending on how much detail you go into.

Paraphrase: to put someone else's idea into your own words.

Quote: to use the exact words of your source.

TIP: FINDING & EVALUATING SOURCES

The easier a source is to find, the less reliable and scholarly it tends to be.

Effort and/or Expertise Needed to Find Source		Quality of Source
Minimal effort No expertise	**Quick Google Search / Wikipedia** You can find a Wikipedia entry in a matter of seconds. It will give you some basic (though potentially inaccurate) information, and your professor will think little of it as a source.	Poor
Minimal effort Some expertise	**More Selective Google Search** With slightly more effort, you can find some material on the Internet that's more reliable—articles from a reputable newspaper or magazine (e.g., the *New York Times* or the *The Atlantic*), even some government documents.	Good to Excellent
Some effort Some expertise	**Books** You'll have to leave your computer (briefly), but if you go to the library or use interlibrary loan, you can find books that explore a topic more deeply and from a more academic perspective. Also, if you go to the library, you can consult with research librarians—take advantage of their expertise.	Good to Excellent
Some effort Some expertise	**Academic Journals** If you want to consult the most academically respected sources, you'll need to find peer-reviewed academic journals. Search for these in Google Scholar (see Chapter 7) and the library databases (see Chapter 9)—they're not always easy to find or search, but the effort is worth it.	Generally Excellent

"Here's what I have to say about that."

This is where you enter the conversation, and essentially you have three options, with some overlap:

- to use the source in support of something you're saying
- to disagree with the source (and offer a different way of looking at something)
- to extend or build upon an idea the source offers

It should always be clear to your reader *why* you're using source material—it should always be in service of something you're developing in your paper.

How much should you quote, paraphrase, or summarize?

The answer to this question depends on a number of factors—the discipline (psychology, linguistics, art history, biology, etc.) you're working in, the type of paper you're writing, and your professor's expectations.

For most research papers, roughly 20 to 50 percent of the paper should come from sources. The other 50 to 80 percent should be you interpreting the evidence and directing our thinking.

Primary vs. secondary sources

Many professors will require that you do both primary (meaning first or original) and secondary research. In the excerpt you're about to read, from Michael Pollan's book, his research on prices of particular items at a grocery store is *primary* research. Most likely, he took notes in a grocery store and/or examined advertising from stores. He didn't rely on some other researcher for this information—he examined the "data" himself. If, however, you use Pollan's book as a source, then his book and everything in it would be a *secondary* source.

Primary sources are often pure data (a government census, enrollment figures at a college, city tax records), but they can also be documents created or recorded by "participants" in an event: letters from Civil War soldiers, video of the Kennedy assasination, etc.

Seconday sources, on the other hand, are those that interpret, comment on, analyze or make arguments about those events: a book that argues how Confederate soldiers became increasingly hopeless as the war progressed, an essay proposing a new theory about Kennedy's death, and so on.

SUMMARIZING, PARAPHRASING, AND QUOTING

These three skills are essential in research writing. I'll cover each one separately, and to illustrate I'll use an excerpt from Michael Pollan's book about food and agriculture in America, *The Omnivore's Dilemma*. The following excerpt appears on page 136, in a chapter that discusses how organic food has become a big industry. With all three techniques, it's important to provide the proper citation For more on citations, see Chapter 10: MLA Documentation or Chapter 11: APA Documentation.

This following excerpt explores how pricing works in traditional supermarkets.

> Wordy labels, point-of-purchase brochures, and certification schemes are supposed to make an obscure and complicated food chain more legible to the consumer. In the industrial food economy, virtually the only information that travels along the food chain linking producer and consumer is price. Just look at the typical newspaper ad for a supermarket. The sole quality on display here is actually a quantity: tomatoes $0.69 a pound; ground chuck $1.09 a pound; eggs $0.99 a dozen—special this week. Is there any other category of product sold on such a reductive basis? The bare-bones information travels in both directions, of course, and farmers who get the message that consumers care only about price will themselves care only about yield. This is how a cheap food economy reinforces itself.

SUMMARIZING

The goal of summarizing is to capture the main idea of the source material—whether it's a paragraph, a chapter or an entire book—as accurately as possible. Remember that your summary must be shorter than what you're summarizing. In this example, I've reduced seven sentences to one:

signal phrase

Pollan asserts that the industrial food economy continues to dominate because neither farmers nor traditional grocery stores are motivated to provide any information beyond price to consumers (136).

You might find it reassuring to know that it took me—the supposed expert in these matters—about five minutes to write that one sentence. I had to keep thinking about which information to include and how the ideas related to each other. I wrote it three different ways before I was satisfied with it.

In a typical research paper, you might use four or five (or many more) sources. Every time you move from one source to another, it's a moment of potential confusion for the reader, particularly when you're also making your own assertions. When you use signal phrases consistently, it helps the reader keep track of who's saying what.

PARAPHRASING

To paraphrase is to put a writer's idea in your own words. Most students go about this in the most counter-productive way: they stare at the original sentence and try to think of synonyms for the key words, then put together a "new" sentence that has different words but often sounds awkward.

Instead, the best way to paraphrase is this:

1. Read the sentence(s) closely and be sure that you understand everything the writer is saying. Pay particular attention to how ideas relate to each other, especially when the writer is showing causality (one thing causing another).
2. Close the book, or the web page, or whatever it is you're reading. Reconstruct the idea in your head in language that makes sense to you. If you're not looking at the original, you'll be less inclined to repeat its wording or structure, and the sentence you write will sound more natural.
3. Start writing, still without looking at the original. Don't worry if you repeat a word or two that appeared in the original.
4. Compare your version to the original. The idea from the original should be intact, but the new sentence should sound like *your* writing. Now, if necessary, think of synonyms to replace key words you repeat from the original.

Here's an example where I paraphrase one of Pollan's sentences. His sentence:

> The bare-bones information travels in both directions, of course, and farmers who get the message that consumers care only about price will themselves care only about yield.

First, I made sure I understood the idea—that farmers have changed their practices *because* (causality) they know what motivates consumers.

This is what I came up with. It might not be the finest paraphrase you'll ever read, but it does the job. The ideas are intact, as is the relationship between them, i.e., the cause and effect. And I believe that the voice is mine, not Pollan's.

USEFUL VERBS

all are better than *says / states*

asserts	**claims**
argues	**suggests**
observes	**maintains**

signal phrase

> Pollan asserts that because many farmers believe consumers are only concerned with cost, the farmers then focus only on how much of any particular crop they can produce (136).

Here's another version, without a signal phrase:

> Farmers who know that consumers are concerned with cost alone will in turn focus only on how much of any particular crop they can produce (Pollan 136).

SLOPPY PARAPHRASE = PLAGIARISM

If you paraphrase badly, you may be at risk of plagiarizing.

First, be sure that you cite your source properly. Yes, even if you put source material into your own words, you still must give credit to your sources for their ideas. If you don't, it's plagiarism.

Second, be aware that if you follow the sentence structure or language of the original too closely, this may be considered *inappropriate borrowing* and thus also a form of plagiarism. For example, the following paraphrase of the Pollan sentence would be deemed unacceptable by most professors:

> Pollan asserts that the basic information moves both ways, so farmers who learn that grocery store customers only care about how much things cost will themselves care only about how much they can produce (136).

Why is this unacceptable? Because if follows the wording of the original too closely. Even though it's properly documented, the language and sentence structure are too similar to Pollan's.

HOW DO YOU DECIDE WHETHER TO QUOTE OR PARAPHRASE?

Your first instinct should be to paraphrase. It's generally better to use your own language—and it's good intellectual practice to put someone else's ideas into your own words.

I'm not saying that you shouldn't quote your sources; quotations are essential, and they can help you be more efficient and accurate. The danger is that when you quote too much, your paper may sound more like a jumble of other writers than *you*.

You need a good reason to quote rather than paraphrase it; here are three:

1. Your source says something in a particularly compelling or interesting way. If the specific language the source uses is important to our understanding of the idea, you should quote that language.
2. Your source says something that is similar to, or supportive of, a point you're making. In this case, the exact words of the source can help back up a claim you're making.
3. Your source says something that you disagree with, and part of your analysis focuses on shades of meaning that can be seen in the precise word choice.

QUOTING

Once you've decided to quote rather than paraphrase, you have one more decision to make: Do you want to quote an entire sentence (or more), or do you want to quote only part of a sentence?

Quoting an entire sentence

This is the easiest way to quote because there are no complicated rules about punctuation. I'll choose a sentence that fits my first reason for quoting—the one that says to quote a writer when he or she says something in a particularly interesting way. Here's what the sentence would look like in my essay:

signal phrase

As Michael Pollan observes, "The bare-bones information travels in both directions, of course, and farmers who get the message that consumers care only about price will themselves care only about yield" (136).

It looks simple, but many students make mistakes with this kind of quotation. It's essential that you have some kind of introduction for the quotation. You should never have a sentence that's only a quotation without any kind of context. (The "context" I've provided above, *As Michael Pollan observes*, is minimal; sometimes you'll want to do more, but generally this is adequate.)

Quoting part of a sentence

This is more common than quoting an entire sentence. It allows you to partially paraphrase a writer's idea but still show his or her exact wording, briefly. Quoting part of a sentence is useful when a writer says something memorable or interesting—or simply difficult to paraphrase—in just a word or phrase. Here I quote part of Pollan's first sentence:

signal phrase

> Pollan claims that stores like Whole Foods use these techniques to "make an obscure and complicated food chain more legible to the consumer" (136).

The key to making the partial quotation work is to write your sentence so that the quoted material flows grammatically within the entire sentence. In other words, if you took the quotation marks away, the sentence would still make sense grammatically—it would still sound like a good sentence. (Though, of course, you wouldn't want to actually do this because that would be plagiarism.)

You can also quote a single word, which puts great emphasis on that word:

> Pollan describes the contemporary agricultural economy as "industrial" (136).

When I was writing that sentence, I had the feeling that I wanted to disagree with Pollan—something about calling attention to that single word *industrial* made me think that the next sentence should question that word choice.

Of course, I could also have emphasized that word because I wanted to assert that Pollan's description is accurate and even revealing:

signal phrase

> Pollan describes the contemporary agricultural process as "industrial" (136); this makes plain the connections between farming and big business and reveals their shared qualities: both are dirty, dangerous, and almost always polluted.

Reminder: This is just a quick overview of the key things you need to know about quoting. In Chapters 10 and 11, I cover additional guidelines that you're likely to need: how to use ellipses (the three dots) and brackets (for words that you change in a quotation), and how to quote someone who's being quoted.

PLAGIARISM

What it is

Plagiarism can take many forms, and some are worse than others. Most simply, it means taking something that is not yours (an idea, a statistic, a piece of research, or an entire paper) and presenting it as your own. This is intellectual theft, and it violates everything that colleges and universities value.

How to avoid it

To begin with, try to find a topic for your research that you care about; I realize that this is sometimes difficult, since many professors choose and/or limit your topics. If you can't choose your own topic, try to find some aspect of the topic that is meaningful to you. When you care about your subject, you're more likely to want to do your own thinking about it.

Plagiarism and research

As you do your research, try to be organized with your sources. Highlight passages that you plan on quoting, paraphrasing, or summarizing. Develop a number or symbol system to help you keep track of sources. I've seen far too many students suffer because they put off doing their in-text citations until they finished writing their papers; this is a terrible idea because at that stage you then have to look up all the page numbers again. Maintain a system as you take notes and as you write. When in doubt, give credit to a source; if you're not sure whether or not you need an in-text citation, provide one.

Don't put the paper off until the last minute. A research paper requires careful attention to detail, and it's generally not the kind of thing you can pull off the night before it's due. It's in your best interest to have all of your citations (in-text and a works-cited page) done in your first draft. That way your professor can let you know if there are problems.

chapter 7

INTERNET RESEARCH

Getting information off the Internet is like taking a drink from a fire hydrant.

~ Mitch Kapor

Everyone knows how to search the Internet, but this chapter is meant to help you search more productively and efficiently—and also to evaluate your results.

Let's say that you're writing a paper that responds to some issue in Michael Pollan's book *The Omnivore's Dilemma* (see previous chapter for excerpt). For the sake of this example, I'll assume that you've narrowed your topic somewhat and decided to address what Pollan calls the "industrial food economy." Of course, the specific focus of your paper will determine how you search, but let's start with some basic principles.

A BASIC GOOGLE SEARCH

The most obvious thing to do is to search for *industrial food economy*, right? Sure, why not…

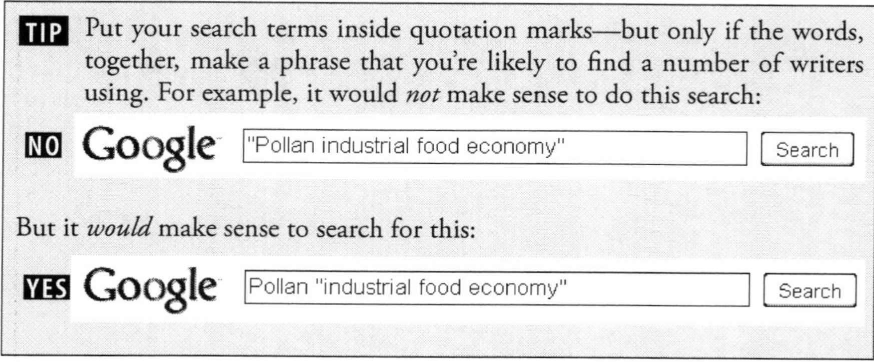

TIP Put your search terms inside quotation marks—but only if the words, together, make a phrase that you're likely to find a number of writers using. For example, it would *not* make sense to do this search:
NO Google "Pollan industrial food economy" Search
But it *would* make sense to search for this:
YES Google Pollan "industrial food economy" Search

In this case, though, for the sake of simplicity and because we want to find things that don't necessarily make reference to Pollan, we'll leave out his name. In the search below, we'll only get results that include the exact phrase *industrial food economy.*

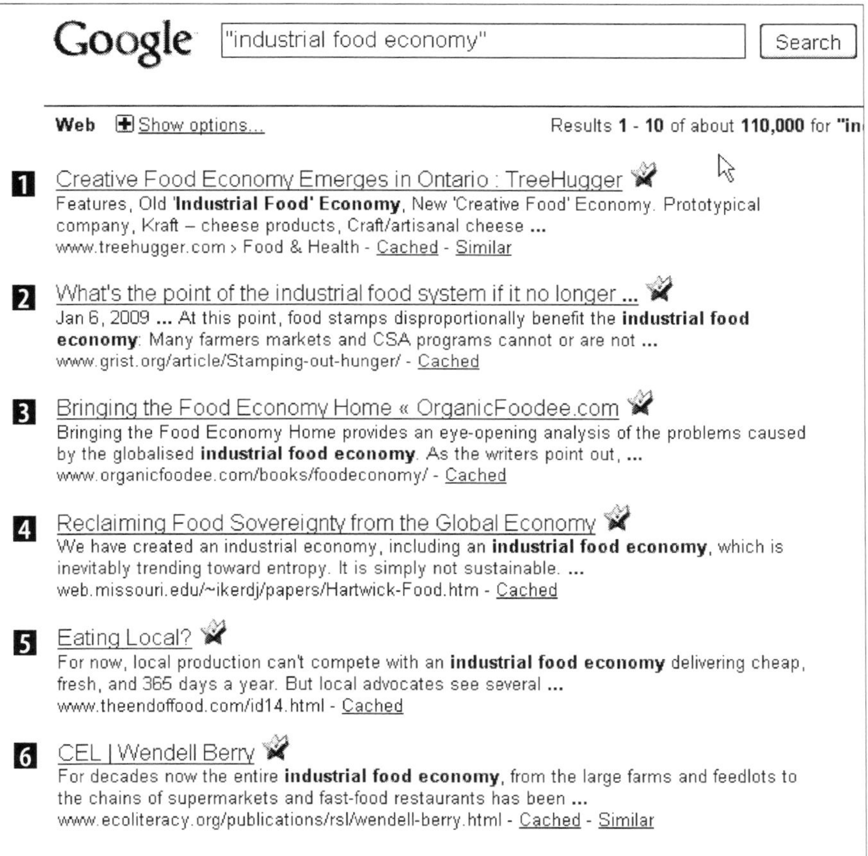

EVALUATING THE RESULTS

This is where things become more complicated, and the best piece of advice I can give you about which sites to consider for your paper is to use both common sense and critical thinking. Let's look at the first result, from TreeHugger.com.

The title is "Creative Food Economy Emerges in Ontario," which makes me think that this probably isn't a great source for a paper, mainly because the focus on Ontario (part of Canada) makes the subject matter too narrow. Also, at the bottom of the page, I can see who publishes the site:

© TreeHugger.com 2010 | Visitor Agreement | Privacy Policy | Discovery Communications, LLC

Discovery Sites: Discovery Channel | TLC | Animal Planet | Discovery Health | Science Channel | Discovery Store Planet Green | HowStuffWorks | Discovery Times | Discovery Kids | HD Theater | FitTV | Petfinder | Turbo

The "publisher" is TreeHugger.com, which means nothing to me. But when I continue reading, I find that the site is clearly connected to the Discovery Channel, which means that it's more about entertainment (and profit) than education or serious research. Hey, I'm not picking on Discovery Channel—I watch it myself and find it interesting and informative. But I wouldn't rely on it as a source for a research paper.

Two sites, compared

Here are the third and fourth results from the search:

> Bringing the Food Economy Home « OrganicFoodee.com - Jan 9
> Bringing the Food Economy Home provides an eye-opening analysis of the problems caused by the globalised **industrial food economy**. As the writers point out, ...
> www.organicfoodee.com/books/foodeconomy/ - Cached -
>
> Reclaiming Food Sovereignty from the Global Economy - Jan 9
> We have created an industrial economy, including an **industrial food economy**, which is inevitably trending toward entropy. It is simply not sustainable. ...
> web.missouri.edu/~ikerdj/papers/Hartwick-Food.htm - Cached -

"Bringing the Food Economy Home" sounds like a reasonably serious title for a page, but the name of the site, OrganicFoodee.com, does not inspire confidence. It sounds informal and casual, not academic or scholarly. The fourth result, on the other hand, "Reclaiming Food Sovereignty from the Global Economy,"sounds more academic. Also notice that the URL is web.missouri.edu, the web site of a large research university. Not every site that ends in .edu will offer reliable information, though, so you should investigate further before you assume that the source will be appropriate.

Let's look at both pages more closely to determine if either of them would be useful as a source for a college paper.

Advertise With Us
Organicfoodee.com
YOUR ORGANIC LIFESTYLE MAGAZINE
Free Organic Newsletter! Sign up here » Search
Home
Top 10 Organics...
Recipes and Books
Ysanne's blog
Chocolate
More Organic Recipes
More Organic Books
10 Ways to...
Herbal remedies
Supplements
Where to Shop
Organic news
Organic sense
Organic stories
Organic inspiration
Organic lifestyle
Organic jobs
About Ysanne
About us
Your emails
Links
« back to list of articles
Bringing the Food Economy Home
by Helena Norberg-Hodge, Todd Merrifield and Steven Gorelick
(ISEC, www.isec.org.uk)
review by Tracy Worcester
Bringing the Food Economy Home provides an eye-opening analysis of the problems caused by the globalised industrial food economy. As the writers point out, this system is only possible because of a whole range of hidden subsidies, and 'it is giving us food that is neither very flavourful nor nutritious, at a price that includes depleted soil, poisoned air and water and a destabilised global climate'. In addition, livelihoods and communities in both the North and South are being destroyed as farmers are pitted against farmers to produce for giant food corporations. Our food economy, in the stranglehold of agribusiness and supermarkets, is 'absurdly inefficient' with many examples of Britain annually importing roughly the same amount of food as it exports. Only through massive subsidies can chemical and energy intensive food carted round the globe be competitive with a local food economy. The consumer pays four times: once at the supermarket till, again through taxes to help farmers compete with the artificially low prices in the global

The fact that the site calls itself "your organic lifestyle magazine" should confirm what I suggested earlier—namely, that it wouldn't be a very reliable source of information. This is not to say that you couldn't learn from the site, or even get ideas for your paper. But it's not the kind of source you want for most college papers. However, if you're writing about how popular concern for organic food has grown, then you might find it useful to examine the popularity and profitability of sites like this.

You should also notice that what appears on this page is actually a review of a book, and maybe the book would be worth reading for your research. In short, even pages that don't look useful can contain something worth exploring. But do so cautiously, and always with an awareness of the quality of sources you intend to use in your paper. Your reader wouldn't take your paper seriously if all of your sources were like OrganicFoodee.com.

Now let's look at the fourth result more closely.

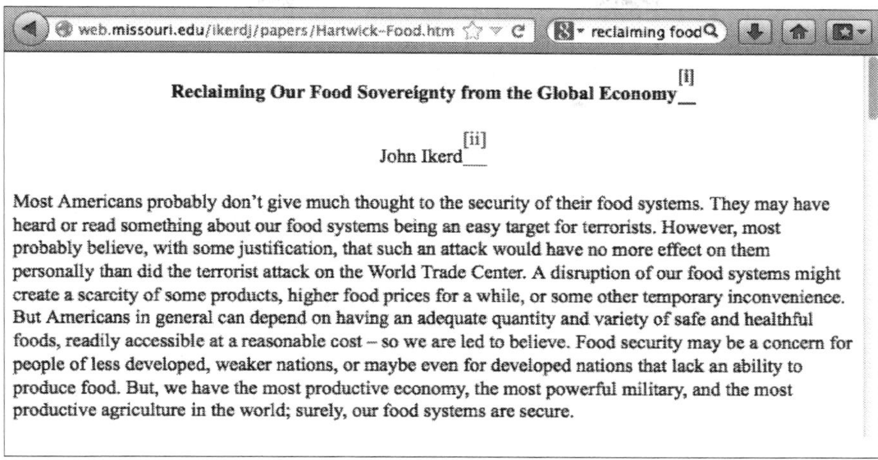

web.missouri.edu/ikerdj/papers/Hartwick-Food.htm

Reclaiming Our Food Sovereignty from the Global Economy[i]

John Ikerd[ii]

Most Americans probably don't give much thought to the security of their food systems. They may have heard or read something about our food systems being an easy target for terrorists. However, most probably believe, with some justification, that such an attack would have no more effect on them personally than did the terrorist attack on the World Trade Center. A disruption of our food systems might create a scarcity of some products, higher food prices for a while, or some other temporary inconvenience. But Americans in general can depend on having an adequate quantity and variety of safe and healthful foods, readily accessible at a reasonable cost – so we are led to believe. Food security may be a concern for people of less developed, weaker nations, or maybe even for developed nations that lack an ability to produce food. But, we have the most productive economy, the most powerful military, and the most productive agriculture in the world; surely, our food systems are secure.

This is just the first paragraph of a long document. Is it a source you could use? How do you decide? There are two key questions that will help you determine how reliable it is as a potential source: Who publishes the site, and who wrote the material you're reading?

Who publishes the site?

We already know that this site is from the University of Missouri. If you go to the bottom of the page, there's no publisher listed—but there is other information that may be helpful.

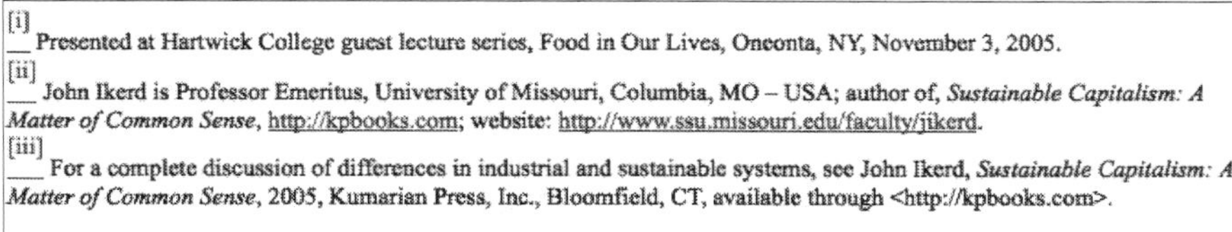

[i] Presented at Hartwick College guest lecture series, Food in Our Lives, Oneonta, NY, November 3, 2005.

[ii] John Ikerd is Professor Emeritus, University of Missouri, Columbia, MO – USA; author of, *Sustainable Capitalism: A Matter of Common Sense*, http://kpbooks.com; website: http://www.ssu.missouri.edu/faculty/jikerd.

[iii] For a complete discussion of differences in industrial and sustainable systems, see John Ikerd, *Sustainable Capitalism: A Matter of Common Sense*, 2005, Kumarian Press, Inc., Bloomfield, CT, available through <http://kpbooks.com>.

The first note tells me that the paper was presented as a lecture at a college, which makes it seem relatively trustworthy.

Who wrote what you're reading?

If you look at the second note, above, you see that the author is a professor and that he has written a book on a related topic. These are both good signs. Again, it doesn't mean that what this paper says is *true*, but it does mean that it's a reasonable source to use in a college paper.

If you're not sure what kind of qualifications the author has, do a Google search and see if you can find out who he works for and where he's been published.

If the sources are all blogs, for example, you should probably rule him out as a serious source. If, however, he's had his work published in reputable newspapers and magazines, he could be a good general commentator on your topic. If he's a working scholar who publishes articles in academic journals, then he's definitely a good source.

Wikipedia?

> Factory farming - Wikipedia, the free encyclopedia
> The issues include the efficiency of **food** production; animal welfare; whether it is ..... **Industrial** production of pigs and poultry is an important source of GHG ... This tells us that dairy farms are good for Pennsylvania's **economy**. ...
> en.wikipedia.org/wiki/Factory_farming - Cached - Similar -

No matter what you search for, it seems, Wikipedia is likely to have an entry. In general, you should use Wikipedia only for background information, and you should verify anything you read there with other sources. (You did know that *anyone* can write or edit almost all Wikipedia entries, right? The obvious result of this very democratic approach is that errors—some created by people to amuse themselves, others because they have some kind of agenda—are common.) Most professors do not want to see Wikipedia as a source in your papers.

INTERNET SEARCHES BY AUTHOR AND TITLE

If you've narrowed your paper topic somewhat, you should have some good search terms already. If you don't, though, here are two suggestions for other ways to search:

Author name: Do a search for the author of anything you've read on your topic. Often, the author has written other works that may explore similar or related subject matter. You'll also find other writers commenting on that author's work.

Work title: This is the same principle as searching for an author's name. If it's a book, you're certain to find book reviews (below), which can be useful.

Searching for the title, *The Omnivore's Dilemma*, brought me to a commentary essay in which the writer objects to Pollan's ideas; it would make a good (though not scholarly) source for a paper on this subject.

> An economist's critique of **The Omnivore's Dilemma**. - By Tyler ...
> Nov 1, 2006 ... In **The Omnivore's Dilemma**: A Natural History of Four Meals, food writer and UC-Berkeley professor Michael Pollan examines three American ...
> www.**slate**.com/id/2152675/ - Cached - Similar

SEARCHING BEYOND GOOGLE

Okay, not exactly *beyond* Google, but beyond the ways most of us ordinarily use Google. This section will introduce you to Google Scholar and Google Books, two great resources that are extremely easy to use.

GOOGLE SCHOLAR

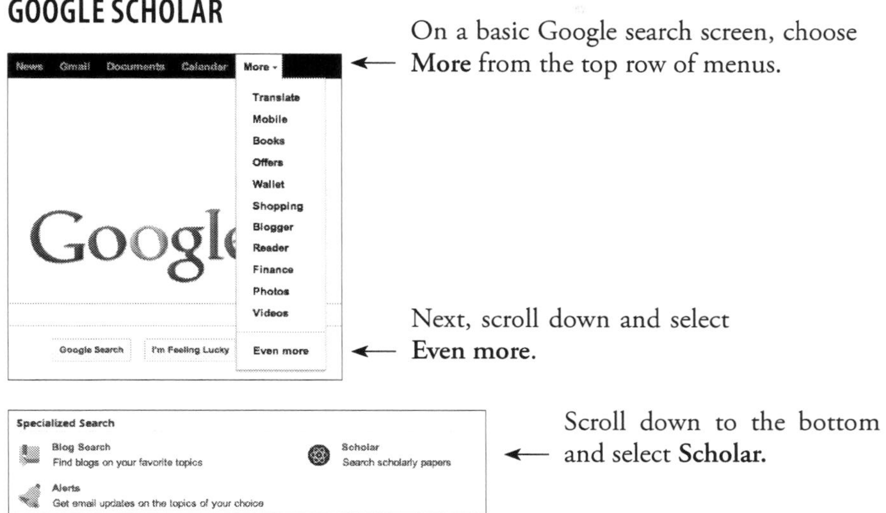

The results that you see on the next page are quite different from the previous searches, mainly in that they're all scholarly articles. These aren't necessarily the only kinds of sources you need in college papers, but they are ones you should learn how to find and use routinely. Quoting from an article in *Time* magazine is fine up to a point, but when you quote from scholarly sources, your reader will take you more seriously.

Google scholar "industrial food economy" Search

Scholar Articles and patents | anytime | include citations

Not in my body: BGH and the rise of organic milk
EM DuPuis - Agriculture and Human Values, 2000 - Springer
... While branded foods have been with us for a long time, economic analysts note that, in this post- **industrial food economy**, branded foods have become the only types of food products large publicly-traded corporations want to own. ...
Cited by 108 - Related articles - BL Direct - All 6 versions

Female identity, fc
CM Counihan - Anthr
Page 1. FEMALE IDE
CAROLE M. COUNIH
Florentine women rev
Cited by 23 - Related

[BOOK] The anthrop
C Counihan - 1999 - t
Page 1. THE ANTHR
Carole M. Counihan F
9BZU-ZHP-SQ19 Pag
Cited by 132 - Relate

RESEARCH TIP

Sometimes when you click on the link, you won't be able to read the whole article. In that case, come back to this screen and try other "versions" (other pages that also have this document). If you still can't find it, note the author and title and search for it in the library databases (see Chapter 9).

Food as Relationship
FL Kirschenmann - Journal of Hunger & Environmental Nutrition, 2008 - informaworld.com
... We often are told that we have a "cheap food policy," which is the cor- nerstone of our quality of life and therefore nonnegotiable. But I would argue that we really do not have "cheap food" in our current **industrial food economy**. There are several flaws in the "cheap food" myth. ...
Cited by 2 - Related articles

[PDF] No Bar Code
M Pollan - Mother Jones. Accessed May, 2006 - chicagoconservationcorps.org
... Even if you count the Organic Supermarket, the entire market for all alternative foods remains but a flea on the colossus of the **industrial food economy**, with its numberless fast-food outlets and supermarkets backed by infinite horizons of corn and soybeans. ...
Cited by 3 - Related articles - View as HTML

Let's look at the fourth result, "Food as Relationship."

Name of journal that published the article
Article title
Author(s)
Food as Relationship
FL Kirschenmann - Journal of Hunger & Environmental Nutrition, 2008 - informaworld.com
... Food always becomes part of the ecology from which it is produced. Page 4. Frederick L. Kirschenmann 109 FOOD IN THE INDUSTRIAL ECONOMY The soil/food/health connection is not the only relationship we ignore in our modern food system. ...
Cited by 2 - Related articles

Unlike a regular Web page, a typical result from a Google Scholar search will take you straight to the article, but sometimes you'll only get an abstract (see below), as is the case here.

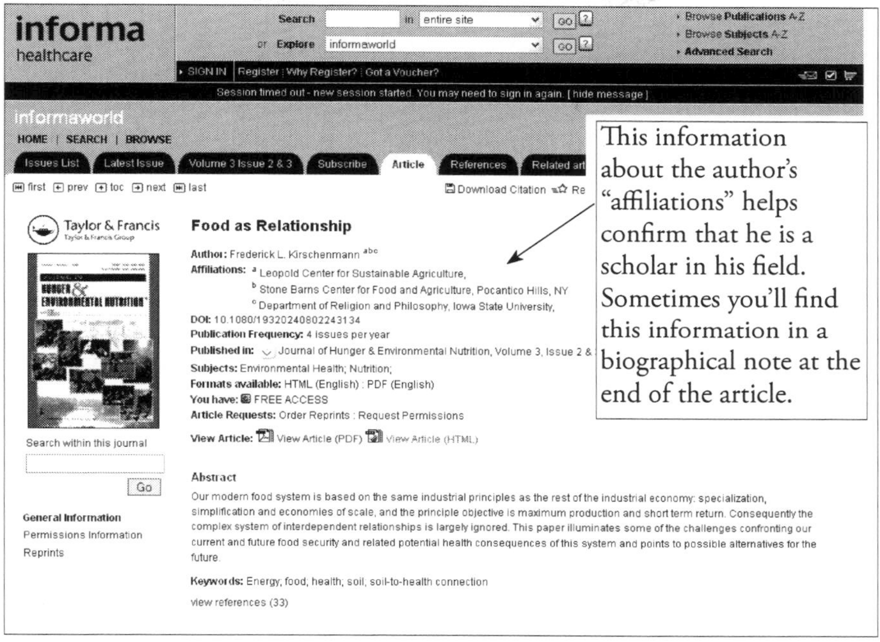

WHAT'S A PDF?

PDF stands for "portable document format," and it means that you're seeing a picture of the original document. One advantage of a PDF is that it's easier to document. See Chapter 10.

WHAT'S AN ABSTRACT?

An abstract is a brief summary of an academic article. It's useful because it tells you, quickly, what the article is about as well as the basic argument the author is trying to make. In the sciences, abstracts also tell you how the author conducted the research.

Reading the abstract should help you decide if you want to read more of this article. If you do, you have a couple of options.

In this case, the site will allow you to look at a PDF of the article, or an HTML (Web) page. Given the choice, always opt for the PDF, primarily because it allows you to document the source more accurately (see Chapter 10).

View Article: View Article (PDF) View Article (HTML)

Here's what the PDF looks like. You can enlarge each page for easier reading or print it. Also note the find box; see instructions on next page for how to use it.

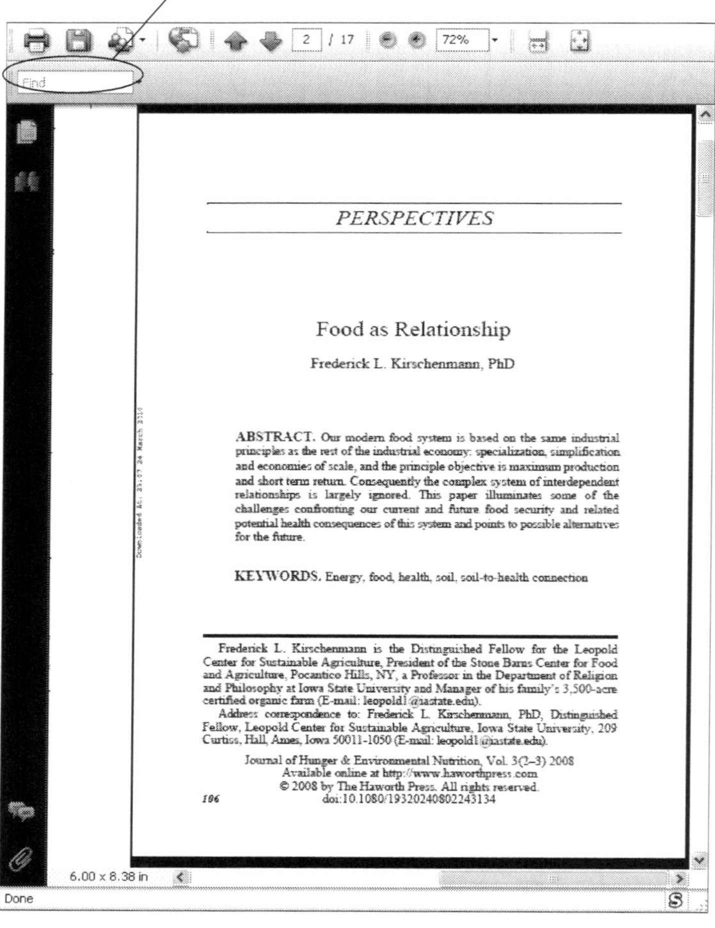

PERSPECTIVES

Food as Relationship

Frederick L. Kirschenmann, PhD

ABSTRACT. Our modern food system is based on the same industrial principles as the rest of the industrial economy: specialization, simplification and economies of scale, and the principle objective is maximum production and short term return. Consequently the complex system of interdependent relationships is largely ignored. This paper illuminates some of the challenges confronting our current and future food security and related potential health consequences of this system and points to possible alternatives for the future.

KEYWORDS. Energy, food, health, soil, soil-to-health connection

Frederick L. Kirschenmann is the Distinguished Fellow for the Leopold Center for Sustainable Agriculture, President of the Stone Barns Center for Food and Agriculture, Pocantico Hills, NY, a Professor in the Department of Religion and Philosophy at Iowa State University and Manager of his family's 3,500-acre certified organic farm (E-mail: leopold1@iastate.edu).

Address correspondence to: Frederick L. Kirschenmann, PhD, Distinguished Fellow, Leopold Center for Sustainable Agriculture, Iowa State University, 209 Curtiss, Hall, Ames, Iowa 50011-1050 (E-mail: leopold1@iastate.edu).

Journal of Hunger & Environmental Nutrition, Vol. 3(2–3) 2008
Available online at http://www.haworthpress.com

106 doi:10.1080/19320240802243134

If you're in a hurry (or just a little lazy) . . .

Let's say you want to find where the author of that article talks about industrialization of food. (This is particularly useful when you find articles that only slightly apply to your area of research.)

Use the **Find** function. On normal Web pages—or any other document—use CTRL + F. In a PDF document, **Find** is at the top of the screen:

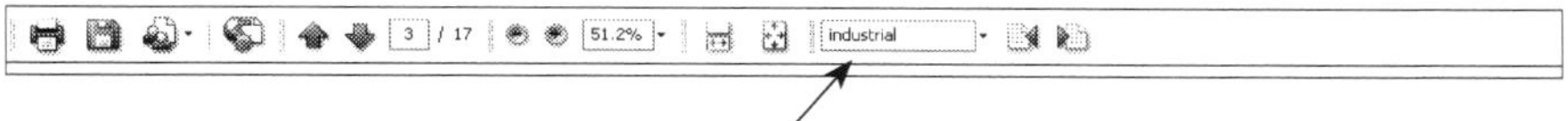

In this case, I put in the word *industrial.* Below you can see one of the places where that word appears. If I hit the ENTER button on the keyboard, it takes me to the next appearance of the word, highlighted in blue.

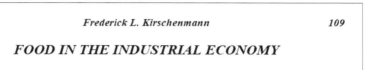

Frederick L. Kirschenmann **109**

FOOD IN THE INDUSTRIAL ECONOMY

The soil/food/health connection is not the only relationship we ignore in our modern food system. In fact, our modern industrial culture tends to view not only food but almost all of reality as a collection of fragments (things) rather than a web of relationships. Modern philosophers trace this tendency to the 17th-century scientific revolution. Rene Descartes wanted science to become a "universal mathematics," which, of course, tended to reduce all of reality to measurable things and ignored dynamic relationships. It should not be surprising, therefore, that we have reduced our understanding of healthy food to an ingredient list.

GOOGLE BOOKS

You won't find the full text of every book here, but you can read large excerpts from quite a few, which makes it a great way to preview books before you decide what you want to get at your library. Click on **more.**

Click on **Books**.

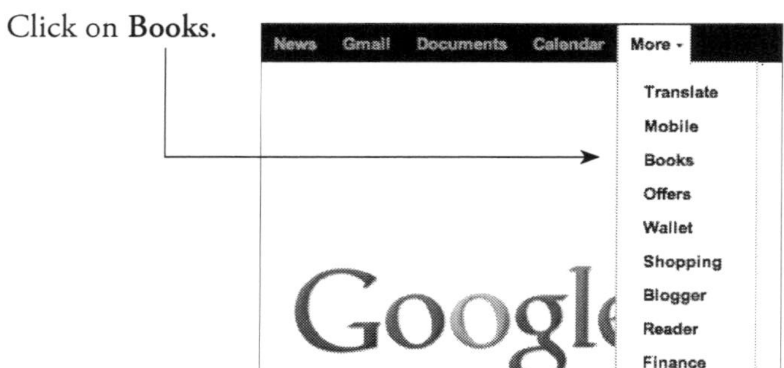

Here are some of the results, using the same search terms as before.

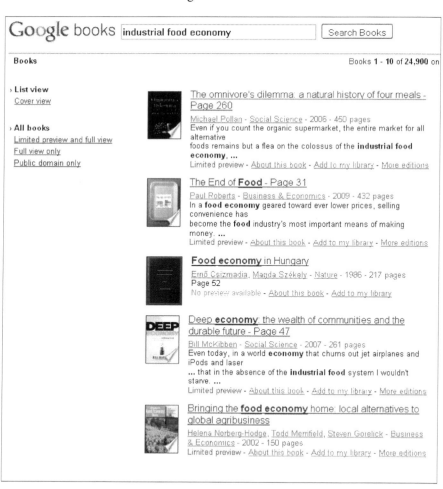

Google books | industrial food economy | Search Books

Books — Books **1** - **10** of **24,900** on

› **List view**
Cover view

› **All books**
Limited preview and full view
Full view only
Public domain only

The omnivore's dilemma: a natural history of four meals - Page 260
Michael Pollan - Social Science - 2006 - 450 pages
Even if you count the organic supermarket, the entire market for all alternative
foods remains but a flea on the colossus of the **industrial food economy**, ...
Limited preview - About this book - Add to my library - More editions

The End of **Food** - Page 31
Paul Roberts - Business & Economics - 2009 - 432 pages
In a **food economy** geared toward ever lower prices, selling convenience has
become the **food** industry's most important means of making money. ...
Limited preview - About this book - Add to my library - More editions

Food economy in Hungary
Ernő Csizmadia, Magda Székely - Nature - 1986 - 217 pages
Page 52
No preview available - About this book - Add to my library

Deep **economy**: the wealth of communities and the durable future - Page 47
Bill McKibben - Social Science - 2007 - 261 pages
Even today, in a world **economy** that churns out jet airplanes and iPods and laser
... that in the absence of the **industrial food** system I wouldn't starve. ...
Limited preview - About this book - Add to my library - More editions

Bringing the **food economy** home: local alternatives to global agribusiness
Helena Norberg-Hodge, Todd Merrifield, Steven Gorelick - Business & Economics - 2002 - 150 pages
Limited preview - About this book - Add to my library - More editions

Not surprisingly, Michael Pollan's book appears first, as he uses the phrase "industrial food economy" a number of times. (I chose not to include the quotation marks in this example because I got better results—I tried it both ways.)

I found the last book potentially interesting, and it immediately struck me as familiar. Then I remembered that this was the book being reviewed at OnlineFoodee.com. Based on the title and subtitle (*Local Alternatives to Global Agribusiness*), I think it could be an excellent source. I might check to see who the authors are, and make sure that it's published by a legitimate company. Being "published" doesn't necessarily make a book reliable, but some publishers are better than others.

I won't be able to read all of this book on Google Books, but I can certainly see enough of it, including the Table of Contents, to know if I want to try to find it at a local library.

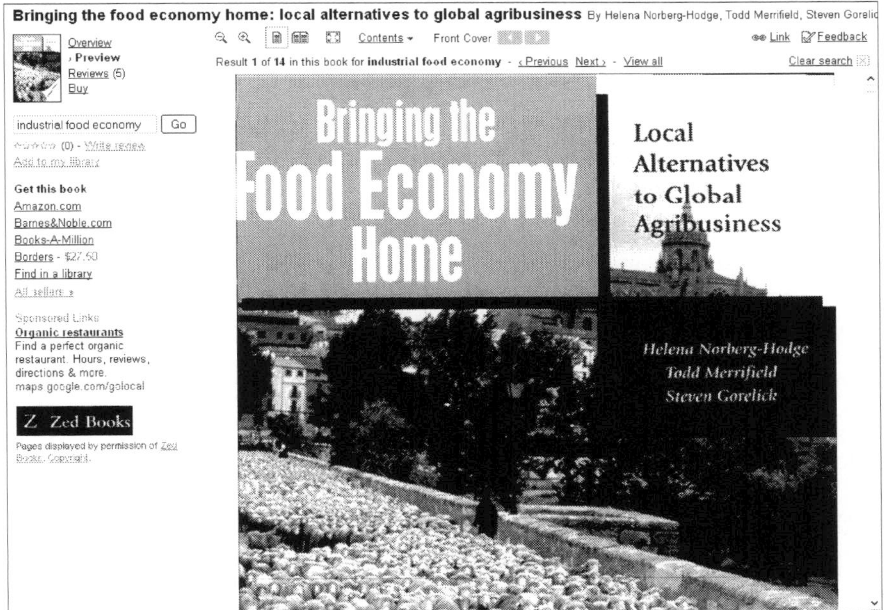

I first click on **Contents** at the top of the page. Here I can see all of the chapter titles.

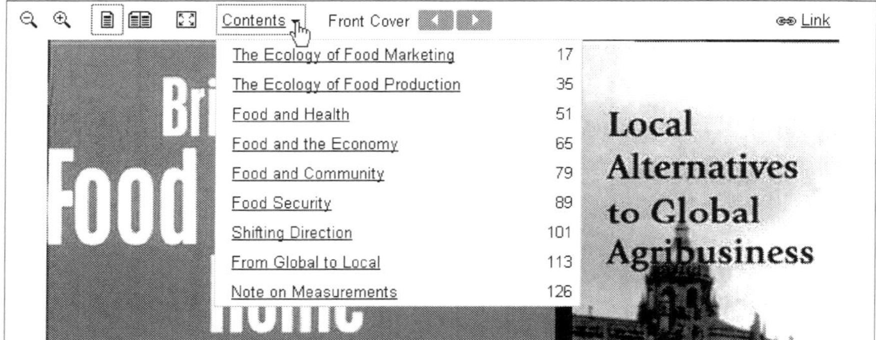

However, when I try to read a few pages into one chapter, I find missing pages:

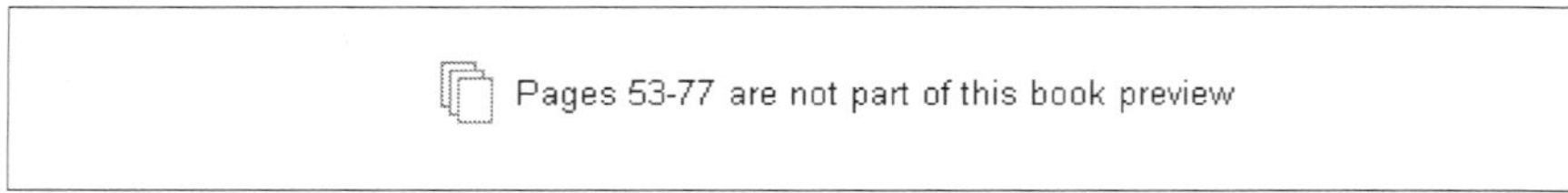

This is pretty common with books on Google. Still, there's a lot of this book that I *can* read, certainly enough to decide if I want to check it out from the library (see Chapter 8: Library Research).

One more tip

Works-cited entries are a great resource for researchers. Many books—not just scholarly ones—will include a list of sources the author used. Michael Pollan's book has an extensive list of sources; these are some he used in Chapter 2:

> In writing about the rise of industrial agriculture I also drew on the following works:
>
> Kimbrell, Andrew. *The Fatal Harvest Reader: The Tragedy of Industrial Agriculture* (Washington, D.C.: Island Press, 2002).
>
> Manning, Richard. *Against the Grain* (New York: North Point Press, 2004).
>
> Morgan, Dan. *Merchants of Grain* (New York: Viking, 1979).
>
> Russell, Edmund. *War and Nature: Fighting Humans and Insects with Chemicals from World War I to Silent Spring* (Cambridge, U.K.: Cambridge University Press, 2001).
>
> Schwab, Jim. *Raising Less Corn and More Hell: Midwestern Farmers Speak Out* (Urbana: University of Illinois Press, 1988). See the interview with George Naylor beginning on page 111.

A "HYBRID" SEARCH

The great strength of the Internet is in linking—the easy movement from one page to the next, where one idea or subject offers an immediate connection to related ideas. To take advantage of this as a researcher, you might want to try what I call a "hybrid" approach, one that combines an online bookstore, Google Books, and your library. I use Amazon.com because it's the largest, but other companies will work too. Start by finding any book related to your topic at the online bookstore. I chose one from the Google Books search.

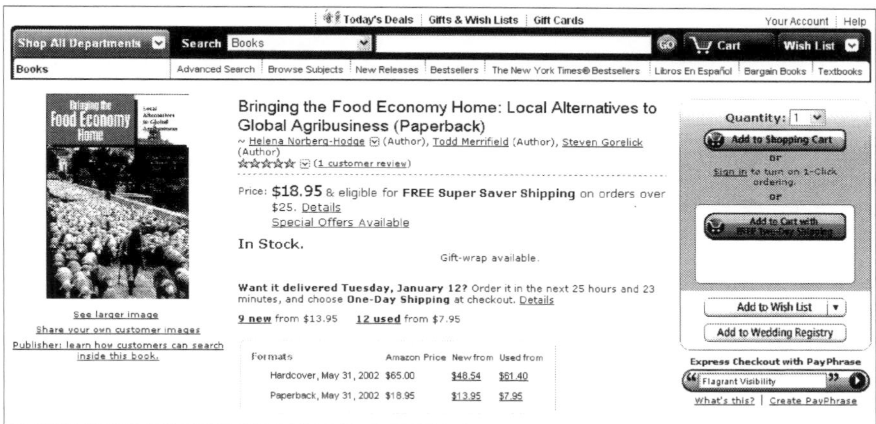

Just a short scroll down the screen you'll find other, similar books. These (and those on the next screen) were bought by customers who looked at *Bringing the Food Economy Home.*

You can also find "tags" (created by customers); clicking on these will lead you to books that have been tagged with specific words, like ***sustainability***.

Explore similar items

Suggested Tags from Similar Products (What's this?)
Be the first one to add a relevant tag (keyword that's strongly related to this product).

Check a corresponding box or enter your own tags in the field below.

food (18) | organic food (9) | dailykos (4)
politics (17) | food safety (8) | sustainability (4)
agriculture (15) | green (6)
sustainable (10) | food justice (5)

Search Products Tagged with

›See most popular Tags

Examing "tags" is also a good way to find some relevant search terms.

The second book, *Recipe for America*, looks promising.

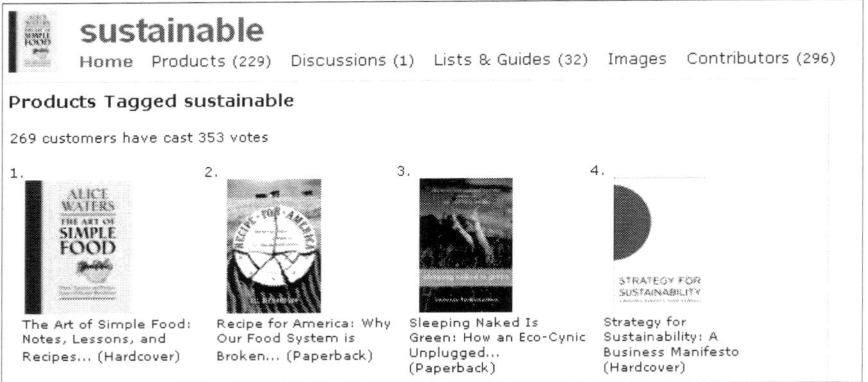

The ***Look Inside*** feature allows you to see the table of contents. But first, you should try to determine whether or not this is a quality source. It gets a high rating from Amazon readers, but you can also see what a professional thinks of it by scrolling down to *Editorial Reviews*.

Click to LOOK INSIDE!
Recipe for America: Why Our Food System is Broken and What We Can Do to Fix It (Paperback)
~ Jill Richardson (Author)
(11 customer reviews)
List Price: $15.95
Price: $10.85 & eligible for FREE Super Saver Shipping on orders over $25. Details
You Save: $5.10 (32%)
In Stock.
Ships from and sold by Amazon.com. Gift-wrap available.
Want it delivered Tuesday, January 12? Order it in the next 12 hours and 20 minutes, and choose One-Day Shipping at checkout. Details

A few pages back, I said that reviews weren't always a great source for your paper; I stand by that. In this case, though, I'm suggesting that you use the professional (rather than reader) reviews to help you decide if the book is appropriate for a college research paper.

This review comes from *Publisher's Weekly*, a respected magazine in the publishing world. It contains some revealing insights into the book. First, the book would appear to be more personal, and not very scholarly, which limits its usefulness somewhat. Second, this reviewer is not impressed by the author's skill in constructing an argument. So it might not be a great source for information or careful analysis. But if you're interested in writing about how the "local food" movement has flaws that largely go unquestioned, this book might be useful.

> Editorial Reviews
>
> From Publishers Weekly
>
> The evils of industrial agriculture are rehashed in this impassioned but sketchy exposé. Food activist and blogger Richardson ticks off a familiar menu of food-system dysfunctions: overreliance on pesticides and fertilizer, exploited farmers and workers, horribly abused livestock, obese children who are fed subsidized junk food in school. . . . Only the choir will be convinced by Richardson's shallow take on these complex issues.

FINAL THOUGHT

The Internet is a powerful tool for research—so powerful, in fact, that you may wonder why we even need libraries anymore. . . . (But we do; keep reading.)

chapter 8

LIBRARY RESEARCH

I find that a great part of the information I have was acquired by looking something up and finding something else on the way.
~ Franklin P. Adams

Who needs libraries when we have the Internet?

Not long ago, if you wanted to do serious research, you went to the library. You searched through card catalogues for books or the *Reader's Guide to Periodical Literature* for articles. Now, of course, you can do similar research from your home computer or even your phone. But there are still good reasons to go to an actual library for some of your research.

Card catalogues at Sterling Memorial Library, Yale University

The first reason is for books themselves. As you saw in the previous chapter, you *can* read parts of some books online. But this option remains imperfect—for many research projects, you still need to go to an actual library to get real, physical books.

And one of the best reasons to go the libary isn't for *what* you'll find there, but *who*—namely, reference librarians. They love helping people find information, and they tend to be very, very good at it. Take advantage of their knowledge and resourcefulness. (You still don't necessarily need to physically go to the library because many colleges also offer live online chatting with reference librarians.)

SEARCHING FOR A BOOK AT YOUR COLLEGE LIBRARY

Building on the previous chapter, let's start with a simple search for a specific author. Go to your college's home page and click on **Library**.

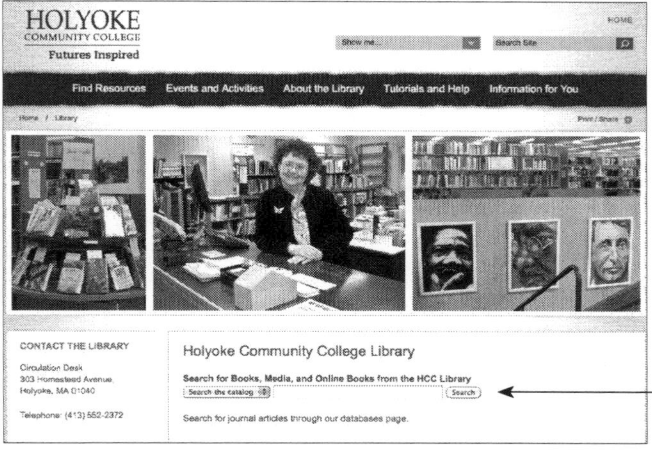

At many libraries, you'll need to select the library catalogue; on this page, however, there's a search field here.

LIBRARY TERMINOLOGY: "THE STACKS"

If the book is available in your library, the call number might indicate that it's in "the stacks." These are the rows and rows (and often, floors and floors) of books on shelves. Be aware that larger colleges may have more than one library—make sure you know which building to search in.

For the sake of this example, let's assume that you want to find a book by an author you're already familiar with, like Michael Pollan.

Start by using the pull-down menu to change the search field from **Keyword** to **Author**.

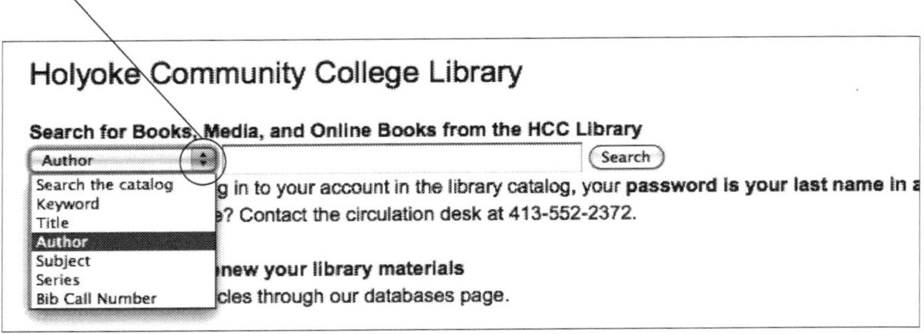

Type in author's name; use first and last name if last name is common; you can type it as *Michael Pollan* or *Pollan, Michael.*

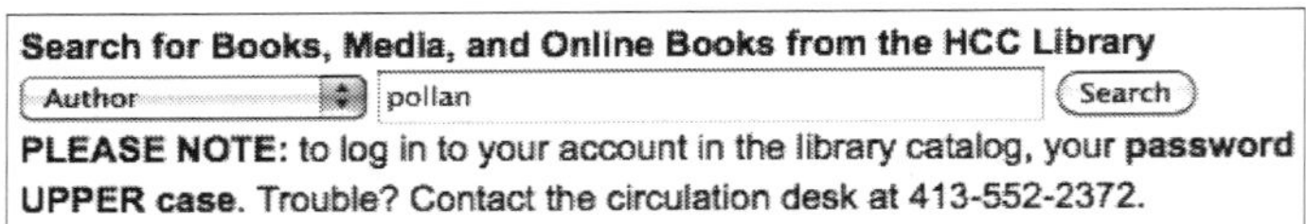

Here are the first three of ten books. Note that in all three cases, it says "1 of 1 copy available at HCC Library."

If the book is not at the HCC library, you can see if there are copies available at other libraries in the system.

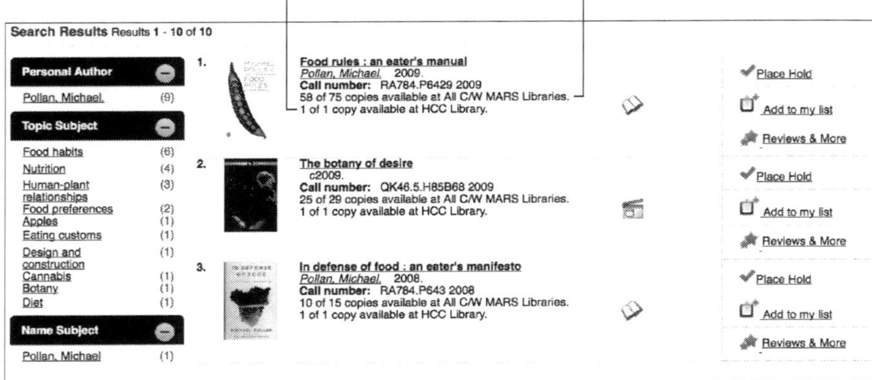

Write down the call number and go find it.

Or, if the book is checked out, request it from another library. by choosing *Place Hold.*

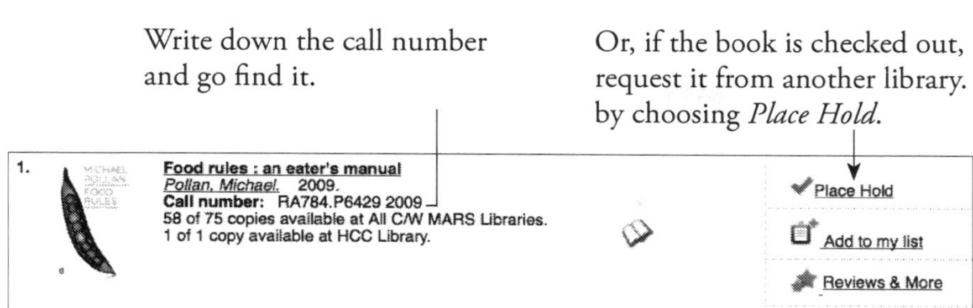

SEARCHING OTHER (OR ALL) LIBRARIES IN YOUR REGION

Let's say you want to find the book that I mentioned in the previous chapter, *Bringing the Food Economy Home: Local Alternatives to Global Agribusiness,* by Helena Norberg-Hodge.

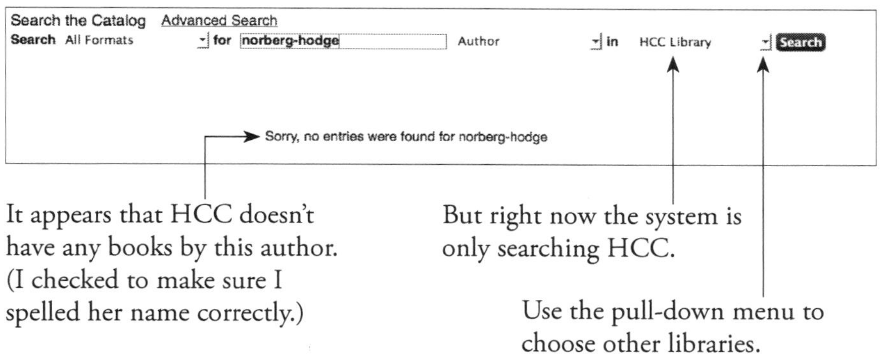

It appears that HCC doesn't have any books by this author. (I checked to make sure I spelled her name correctly.)

But right now the system is only searching HCC.

Use the pull-down menu to choose other libraries.

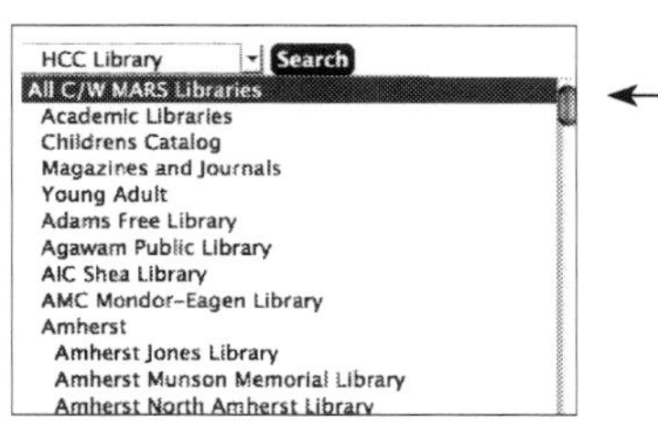

You can check another library, or, better still, tell the system to look in all the libraries in your region by selecting *All C/W MARS Libraries.* (In most library catalogues, the option for searching all libraries in the system will be either first or last in the pull-down menu. In this case, it's first.)

The search returned five results; here's the book I was looking for:

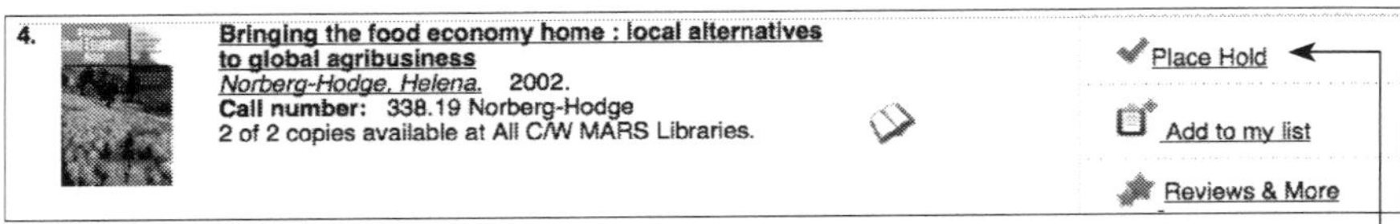

If you click on the book title on this screen, the next page will tell you which libraries have the book; if one of those is convenient for you, simply go there and check it out. Otherwise, request that it be sent to you by placing a hold.

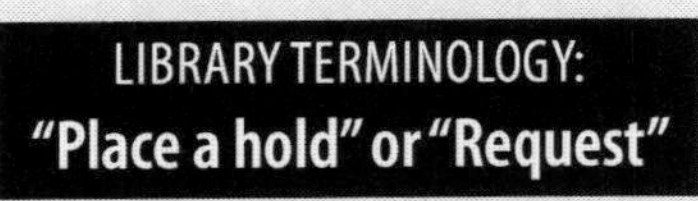

This is how you get a book that's in your system but not in a library that's convenient for you to go to. Usually, it takes only a few days to receive a book after requesting it. With a new or popular book, however, other people may have requested it too, which means that you'll have to wait; in cases like this, it can take weeks or months before you actually get the book.

USING ADVANCED AND KEYWORD SEARCHES

Keyword searches in library catalogues have improved a great deal over the last few years, but they're still not quite like a Google search. For example, I did a keyword search in our library system for *industrial food economy*; I got 82 results, but 17 of the first 20 books were about travel, not food (*Mali in Pictures, Discover Sudan*, etc.). When I switched to an Advanced Search, the results were far better.

Switch to Advanced Search. Search all libraries in region.

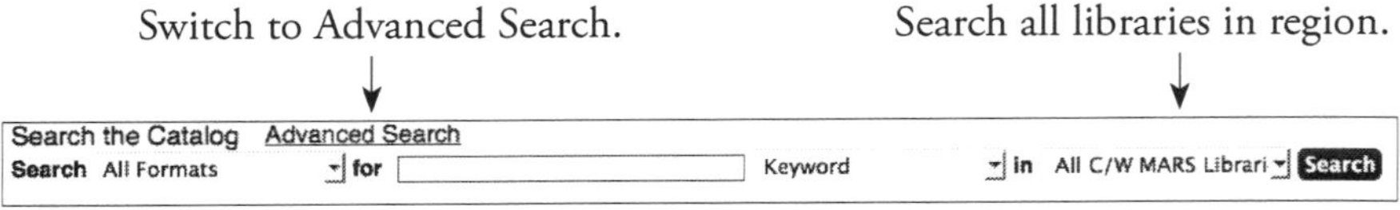

With an advanced search, you can choose multiple keyword fields; put words in two, three, or more fields to get increasingly specific results. If you don't get good results, try using only one or two search terms.

You can also add search rows.

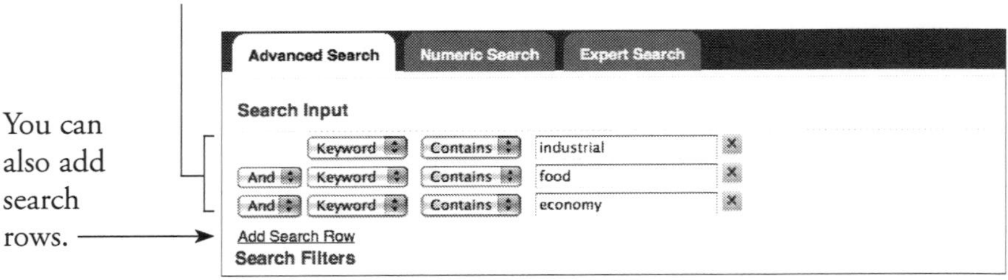

With the exception of the first book, all of the results on the first page were directly relevant to the topic. (Below are just the first six.)

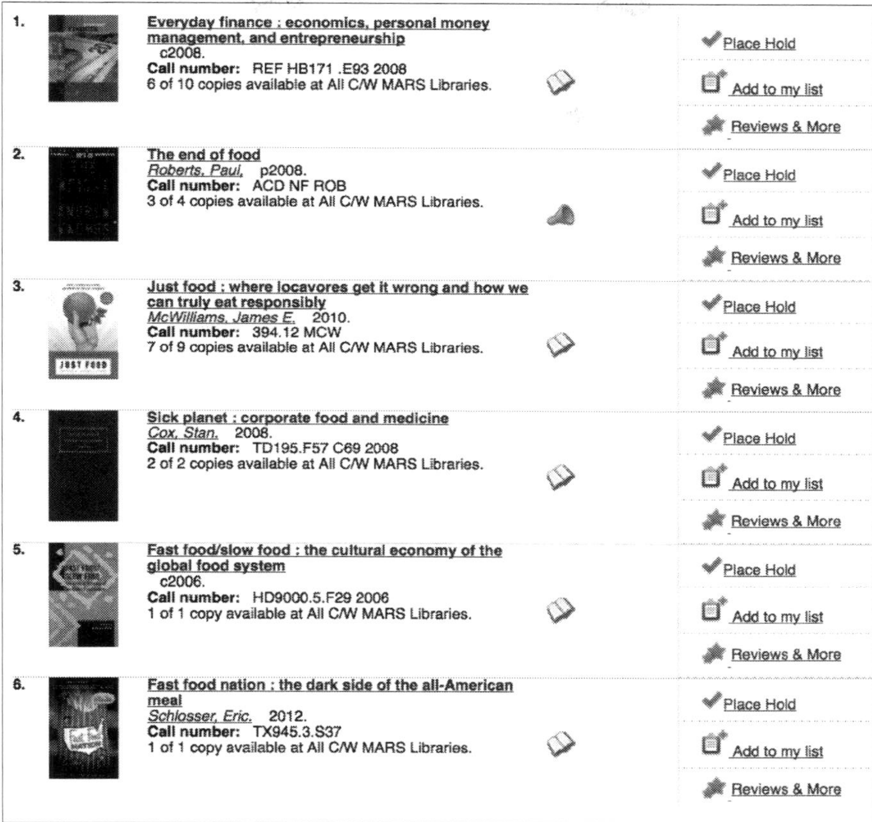

To the left of the search results you'll find this box. ⟶

Topic Subject

Food industry and trade	(11)
Economic aspects	(8)
History	(7)
Economic conditions	(5)
Social aspects	(5)
Food supply	(5)
Environmental aspects	(5)
Globalization	(5)
Food habits	(4)

It offers a number of different subject headings related to your search. If you click on some of these, you'll find books that tend to be closely related to your search.

Many books are also offered electronically—you can view (or download) the book and read it instantly. The electronic version looks better than most books in Google Books (the page is cleaner looking), and it has a number of search tools, making it a great resource for research.

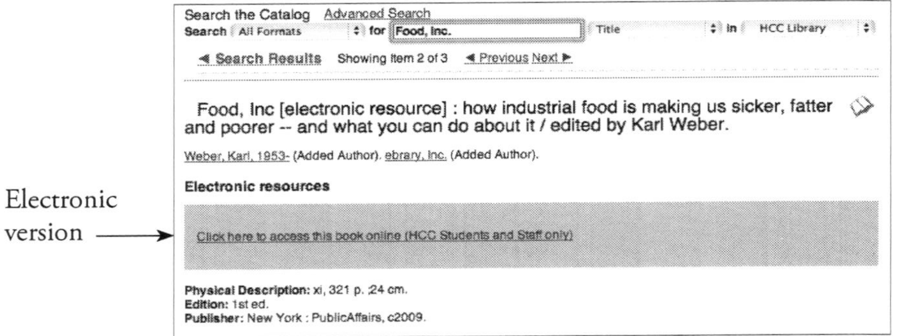

The final word

Searching in the library catalogue is becoming more and more like searching the Internet—but without all the pop-ups, viruses, broken links, etc. It tends to have fewer images, so it's less graphically pleasing. But don't you have enough images everywhere else in your browsing life?

chapter 9

DATABASE RESEARCH

Knowing a great deal is not the same as being smart; intelligence is not information alone but also judgment, the manner in which information is collected and used.

~ Carl Sagan

Not long ago, college and university libraries were judged by their "holdings," i.e., how many books, journals, and other materials they owned. Students who attended big, prestigious universities had a distinct advantage over, say, community college students because well-funded libraries had significantly bigger collections. If you wanted an article from the *Journal of Personality and Social Psychology* from the spring of 1966, you could probably find it at a big university—but not at a smaller college library.

By the 1980s, microfiche and microfilm allowed researchers to look at many more articles (magnified from tiny spools of film inside large, hot projector-like machines). These devices improved research for many students, but they were nowhere near as powerful as the one resource available to every college student today: *databases*.

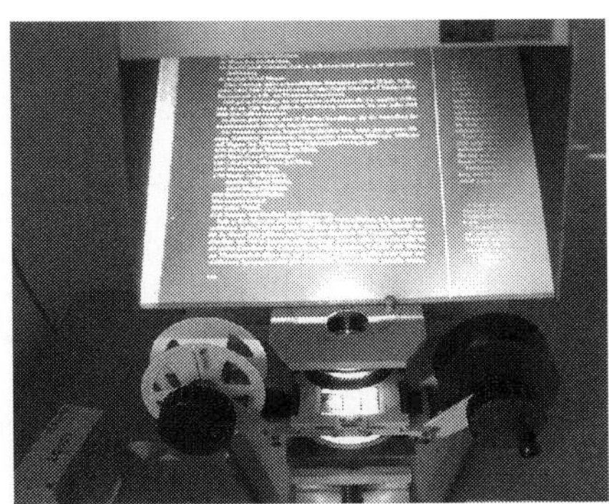

Microfilm machine

These vast digitized storehouses hold more than *one hundred million* articles, images and other research materials.

Databases have everything from a recent *NPR* podcast (with transcript) on Google Glass . . .

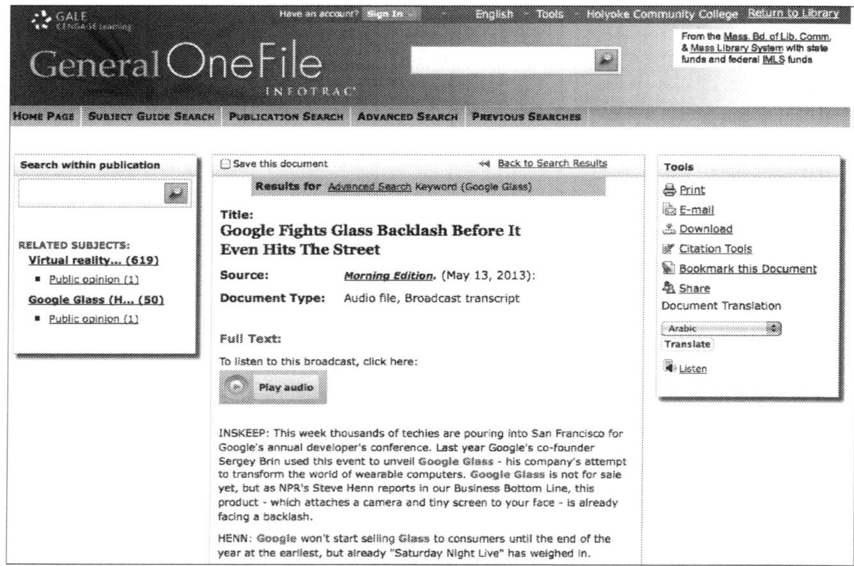

. . . to *New York Times* editorials from 1860 discussing the possibility of a Lincoln presidency.

More Disunion Nonsense.
New York Times (1857-1922); Aug 11, 1860;
ProQuest Historical Newspapers The New York Times (1851 - 2006)
pg. 4

More Disunion Nonsense.

The Charleston *Mercury* the other day said that LINCOLN would certainly be elected, unless the North could be made to believe that in such an event the South would dissolve the Union. In the effect of this menace the *Mercury* places its last hope of defeating the Republican candidate. Southern Pro-Slavery Democrats evidently take the same view of the case, and are trying to act upon it. They have planned a regular political campaign, based on making the North *believe* that Disunion will follow LINCOLN's election. A Commit-

Databases are an amazing storehouse of valuable research materials. Yet very few students take advantage of them, primarily because—at least compared to the Internet—databases are harder to find and more challenging to use, at least at first.

WHAT IS A DATABASE?

A database is a collection of articles (and other materials) from magazines, newspapers, encyclopedias, and scholarly journals. Some databases are general, like the one called "General OneFile," where I found that *NPR* piece. Others are more specialized, like the *New York Times* Historical database, where the Lincoln editorial came from. There are databases devoted just to nursing, education, veterinary medicine, and many other fields. Generally, databases are available only by subscription; your college pays a considerable amount of money so that you can have access to these materials.

HOW DO YOU GET TO THE DATABASES?

Most college students will get to the databases via their college library's web page, which means first going to the college homepage. From there, the method of accessing the databases will vary. Below I demonstrate how it works at my college. If your college's site is confusing, ask a librarian for directions.

Go to your college's home page and click on **Library**.

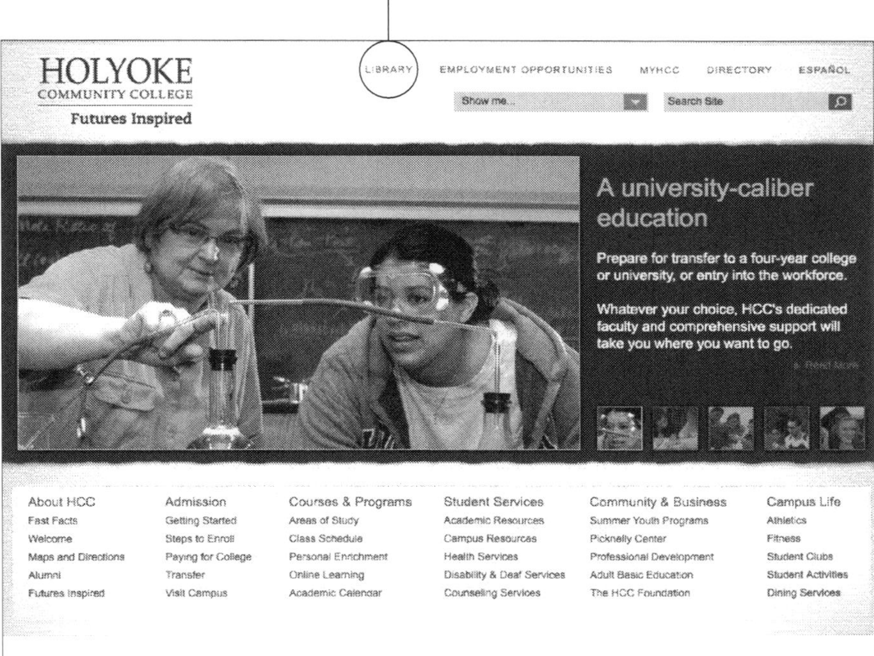

On the Library homepage, choose **Find Resources** or scroll down to . . .

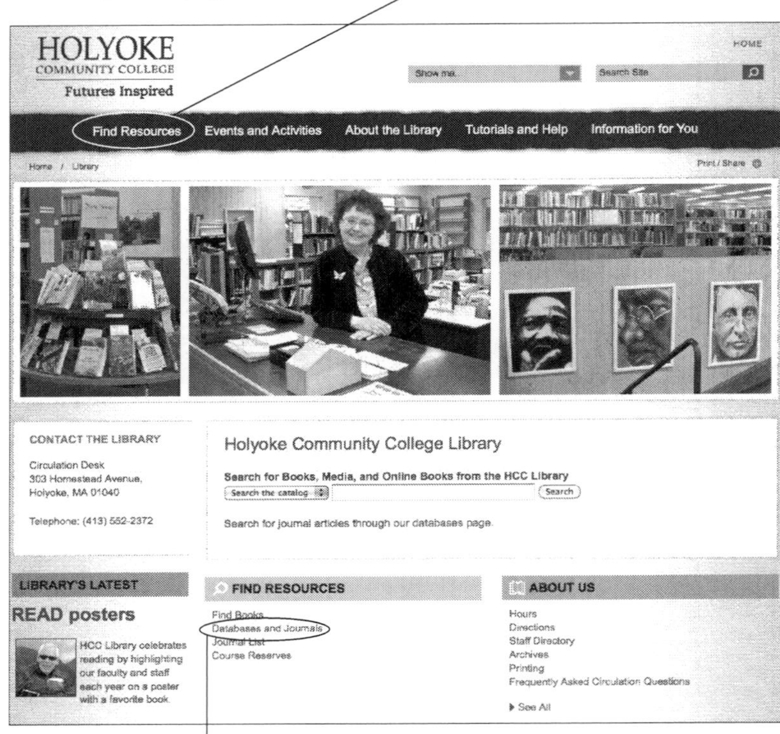

. . . **Databases and Journals.**

I recommend starting with *General Databases (Popular)*. For more scholarly research, try the *Scholarly & Academic* option.

Note also that you can search by field; this may be useful in future courses.

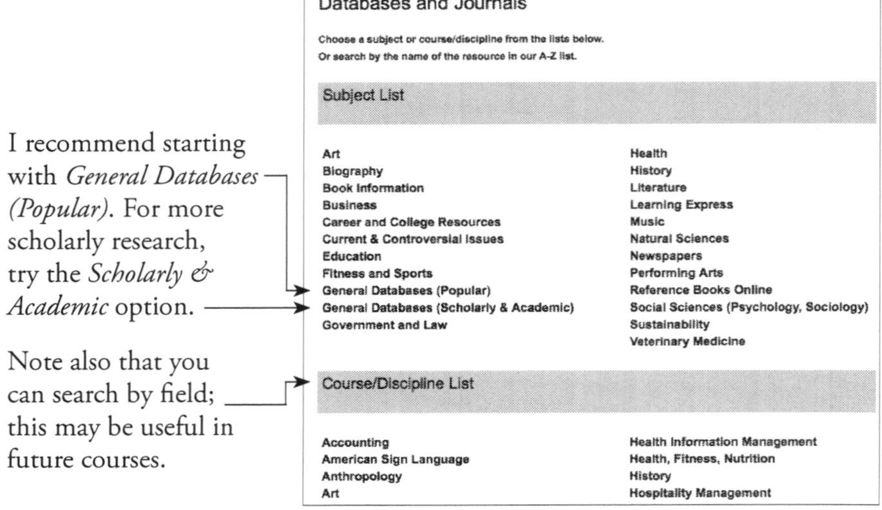

The databases in the image below may look different when you access them, so if you don't find the one you want, scroll down the page to see the full list.

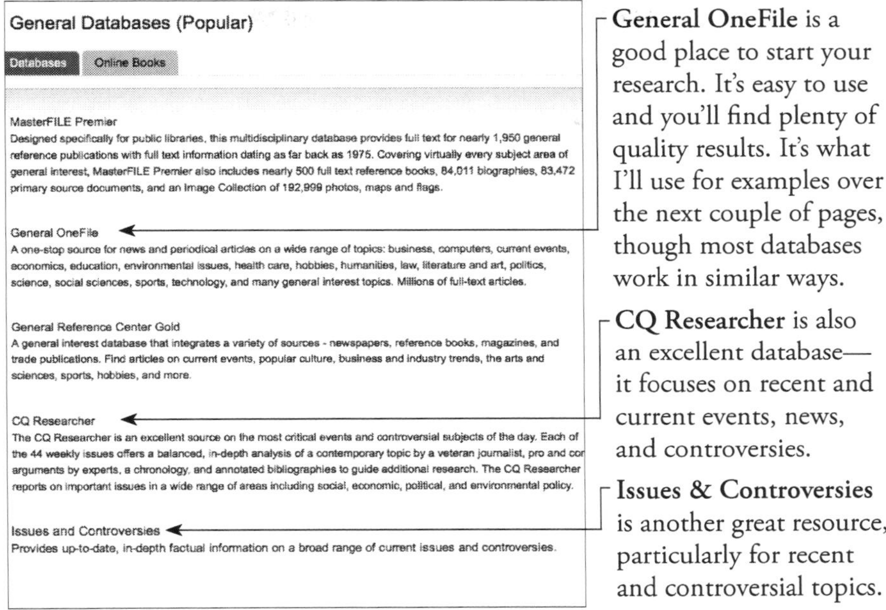

A BASIC DATABASE SEARCH

Most databases use a basic keyword search as a default, so we'll start here.

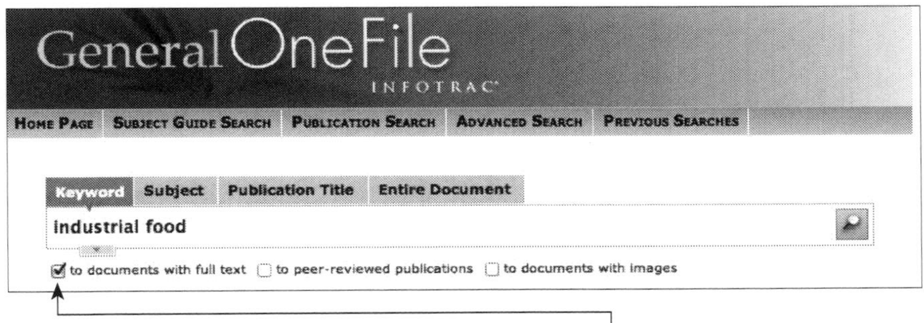

By checking this box, I limit the results **to documents with full text.** This way, I'll be able to read all of the articles now. (For more advanced research, you may not want to check this box.)

To begin, I use the term *industrial food* in the search field. I tried a few different variations, such as adding the word economy (as I did in previous chapters), but this combination worked best. The lesson? Experiment.

However, even with good search terms, I didn't immediately get good results. As you can see from the titles below, these articles don't seem particularly useful.

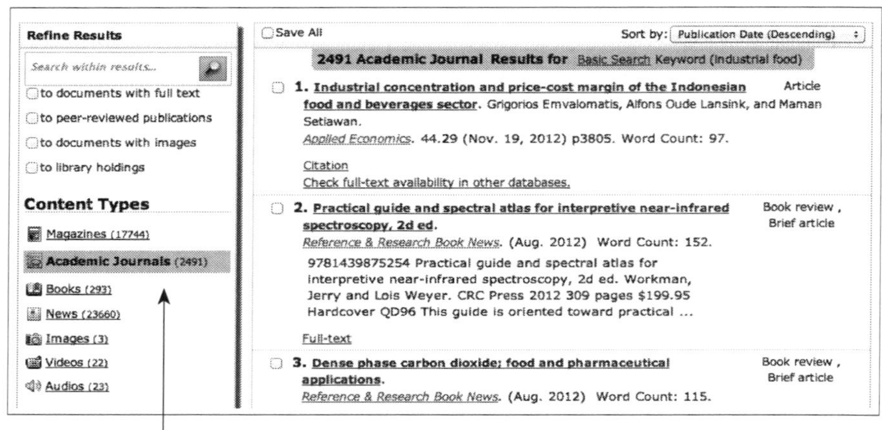

Note: The system first shows you results from **academic journals**. This may be what you want, or you may want to change it to **magazines** if you're just getting started with your research and want material that's easier to read.

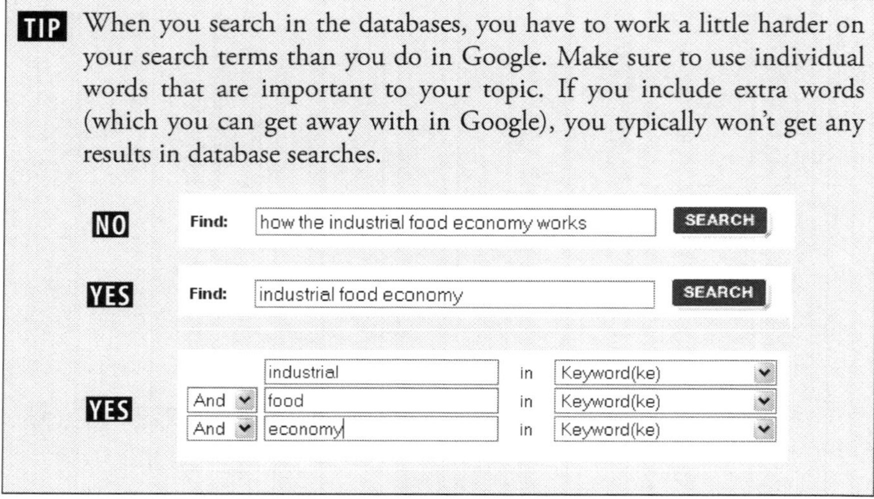

TIP When you search in the databases, you have to work a little harder on your search terms than you do in Google. Make sure to use individual words that are important to your topic. If you include extra words (which you can get away with in Google), you typically won't get any results in database searches.

If you get results that don't seem relevant to your research, change the way the database displays the results. By default, it shows you articles in order of how recently they were published: **Publication Date (Descending)**.

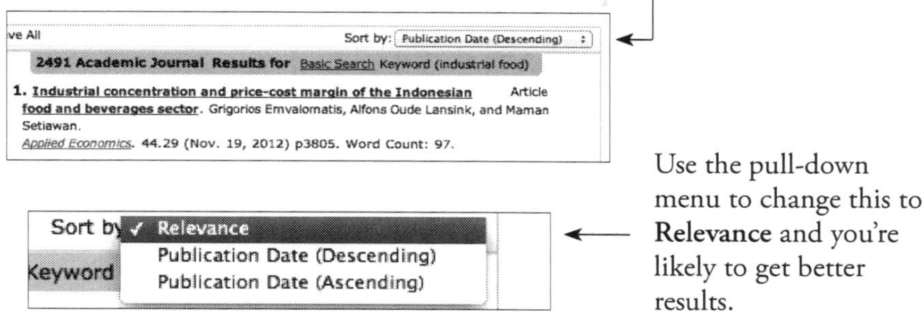

Use the pull-down menu to change this to **Relevance** and you're likely to get better results.

Below are the new results, which are far more useful. Also, I added a limiting search term (farms) here to get even more specific results.

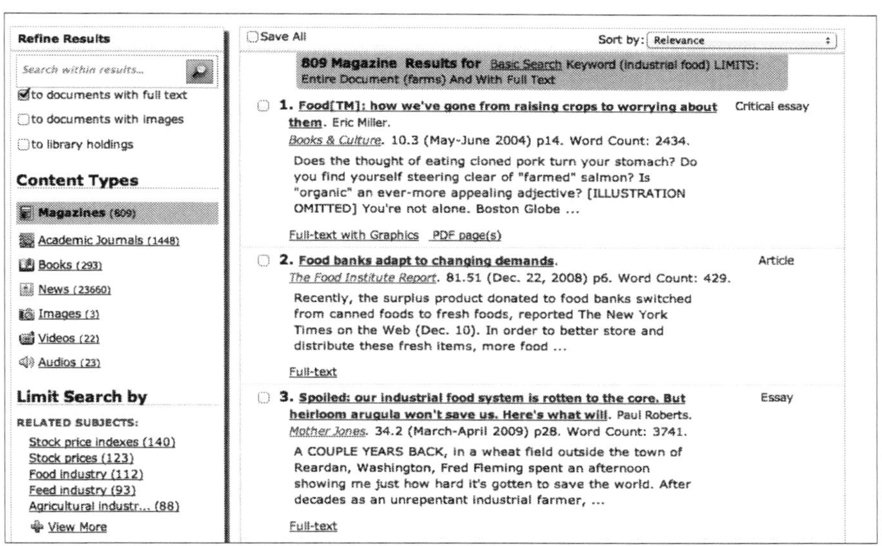

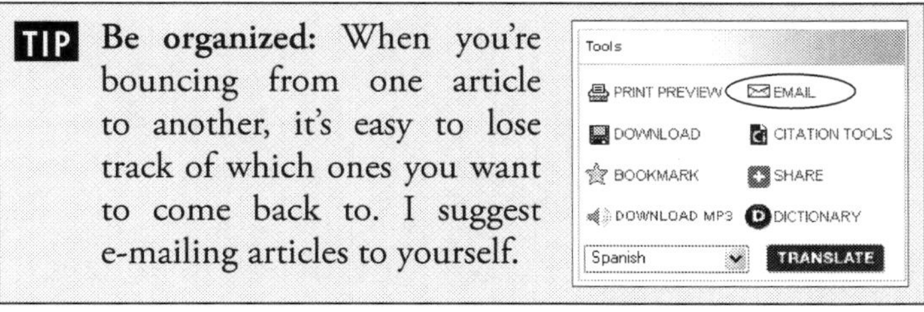

TIP **Be organized:** When you're bouncing from one article to another, it's easy to lose track of which ones you want to come back to. I suggest e-mailing articles to yourself.

The article below was the fifth result for magazines. I chose it for two reasons. First, I like the title because it expresses a strong viewpoint. (Click on it to read the article.) Second, I'm familiar with this magazine, *Mother Jones*, and know that it's a reliable source.

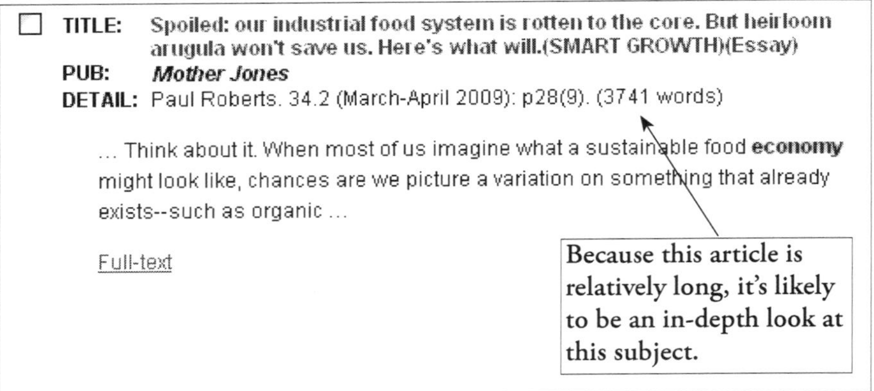

TITLE: Spoiled: our industrial food system is rotten to the core. But heirloom arugula won't save us. Here's what will.(SMART GROWTH)(Essay)
PUB: Mother Jones
DETAIL: Paul Roberts. 34.2 (March-April 2009): p28(9). (3741 words)
... Think about it. When most of us imagine what a sustainable food economy might look like, chances are we picture a variation on something that already exists--such as organic ...
Full-text
Because this article is relatively long, it's likely to be an in-depth look at this subject.

PEER-REVIEWED PUBLICATIONS

For some papers, you'll want to find legitimate scholarly materials: articles that have been published in academic journals that are *peer-reviewed*. When an article is peer-reviewed, it means that—before the article is published—other scholars have read the article and determined that it meets the standards of their field. For example, I am an editor for a peer-reviewed journal; last year, a peer reviewer read an article we were considering publishing and suggested that the writer needed to familiarize herself with certain research that was relevant to her topic. We didn't publish the article until the peer reviewer was satisfied with the quality of the research.

Although peer-reviewed articles are regarded as the most reliable and trustworthy sources available, it's worth remembering that peer review does not guarantee that the article will be true, or that there are not other legitimate ways of thinking about a subject.

Check this box to limit the results **to peer-reviewed publications.**

RESEARCHING CONTROVERSIAL ISSUES

The world supplies us with unending controversy about all manner of subjects. I recommend *CQ Researcher* and *Opposing Viewpoints in Context* (you can find them both under the "General Databases").

The first one, *CQ Researcher*, offers lengthy articles introducing a range of compelling topics. For example, I simply used *technology* as a search term, and these were the results:

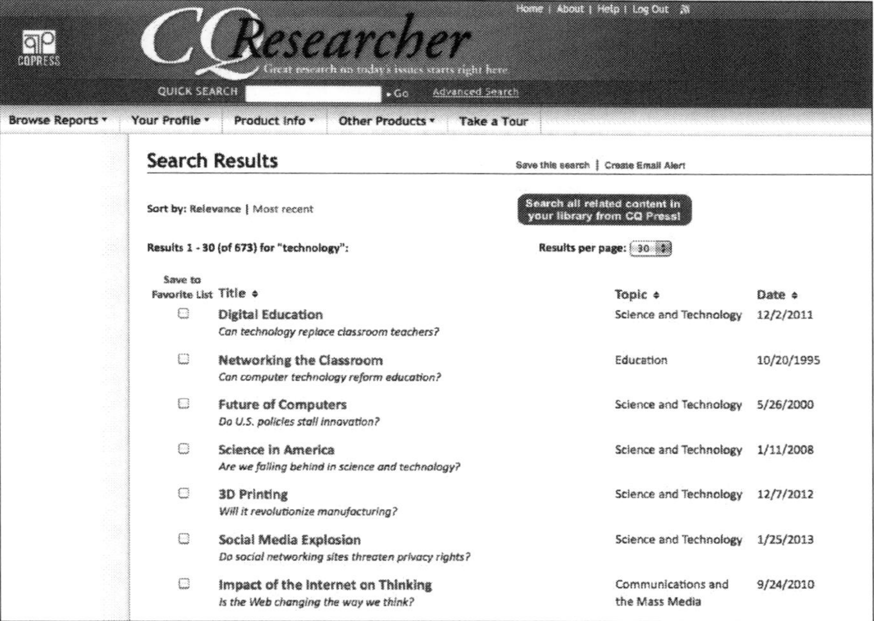

I read some of a number of these articles—all of them are quite long and go into a great deal of depth. It's worth remembering, though, that these "articles," while well-researched, are written by reporters, not by experts in these fields. Still, they are a very good place to start your research and learn the basic positions and viewpoints surrounding a controversial issue.

TIP When it comes to database searches, the single most important thing you can do is experiment. I've barely begun to describe what these databases can do—start clicking on things and find out. . . .

The other database, *Opposing Viewpoints in Context*, has quite a few topics on its front page and can help you find a direction for your research.

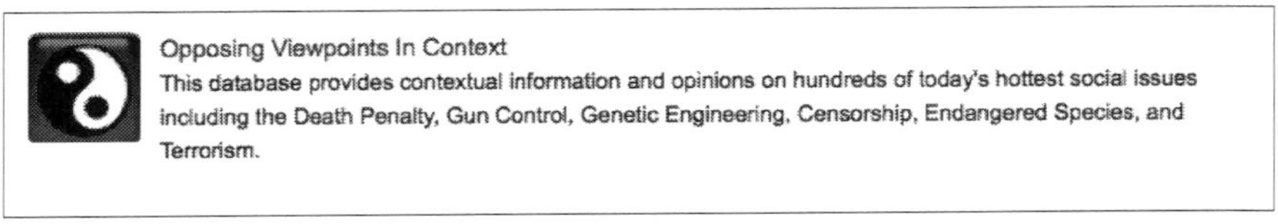

Opposing Viewpoints In Context
This database provides contextual information and opinions on hundreds of today's hottest social issues including the Death Penalty, Gun Control, Genetic Engineering, Censorship, Endangered Species, and Terrorism.

Below are just some of the topics you can find in this database.

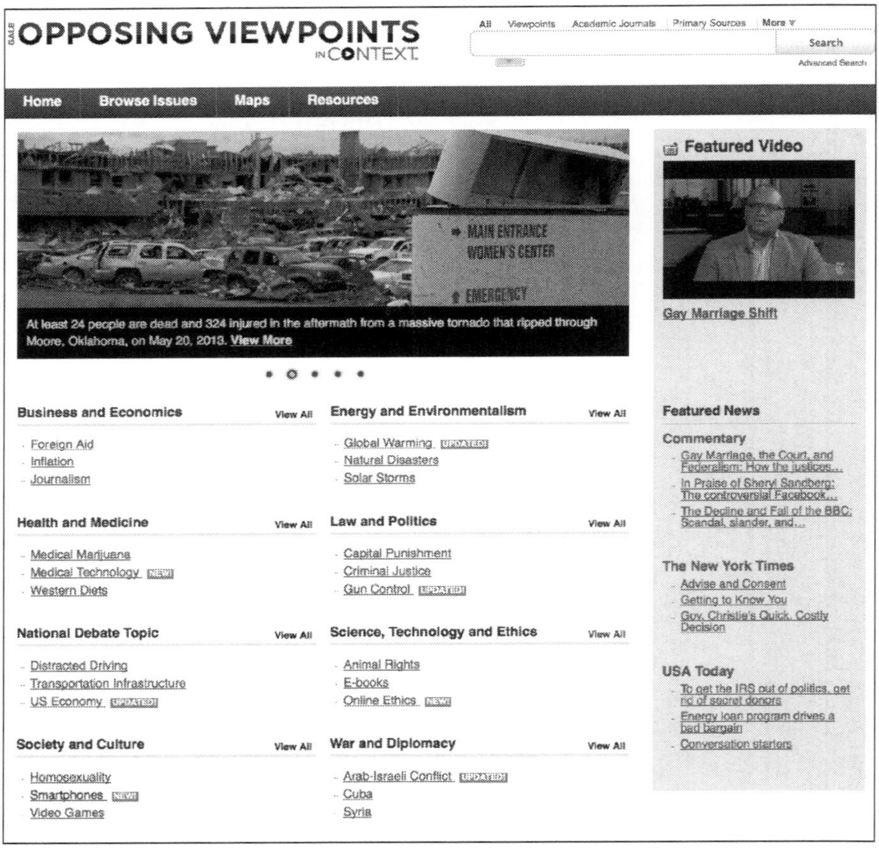

GALE OPPOSING VIEWPOINTS IN CONTEXT

All | Viewpoints | Academic Journals | Primary Sources | More

Search

Advanced Search

Home | Browse Issues | Maps | Resources

At least 24 people are dead and 324 injured in the aftermath from a massive tornado that ripped through Moore, Oklahoma, on May 20, 2013. View More

Business and Economics View All
- Foreign Aid
- Inflation
- Journalism

Energy and Environmentalism View All
- Global Warming UPDATED!
- Natural Disasters
- Solar Storms

Health and Medicine View All
- Medical Marijuana
- Medical Technology NEW!
- Western Diets

Law and Politics View All
- Capital Punishment
- Criminal Justice
- Gun Control UPDATED!

National Debate Topic View All
- Distracted Driving
- Transportation Infrastructure
- US Economy UPDATED!

Science, Technology and Ethics View All
- Animal Rights
- E-books
- Online Ethics NEW!

Society and Culture View All
- Homosexuality
- Smartphones NEW!
- Video Games

War and Diplomacy View All
- Arab-Israeli Conflict UPDATED!
- Cuba
- Syria

Featured Video

Gay Marriage Shift

Featured News

Commentary
- Gay Marriage, the Court, and Federalism: How the justices...
- In Praise of Sheryl Sandberg: The controversial Facebook...
- The Decline and Fall of the BBC: Scandal, slander, and...

The New York Times
- Advise and Consent
- Getting to Know You
- Gov. Christie's Quick, Costly Decision

USA Today
- To get the IRS out of politics, get rid of secret donors
- Energy loan program drives a bad bargain
- Conversation starters

From the main page, I chose *Science, Technology and Ethics*. On the next page, where I found more than forty additional subdivisions of that topic, I chose *Technology and Education*.

What's interesting about this page is the variety of ways the content is organized. Under *Featured Viewpoints*, the articles represent a range of views on current topics. Under *Academic Journals*, you'll find more scholarly articles.

Not all of these articles are as relevant or scholarly as I'd like them to be, but the database as a whole is a solid way to begin your research.

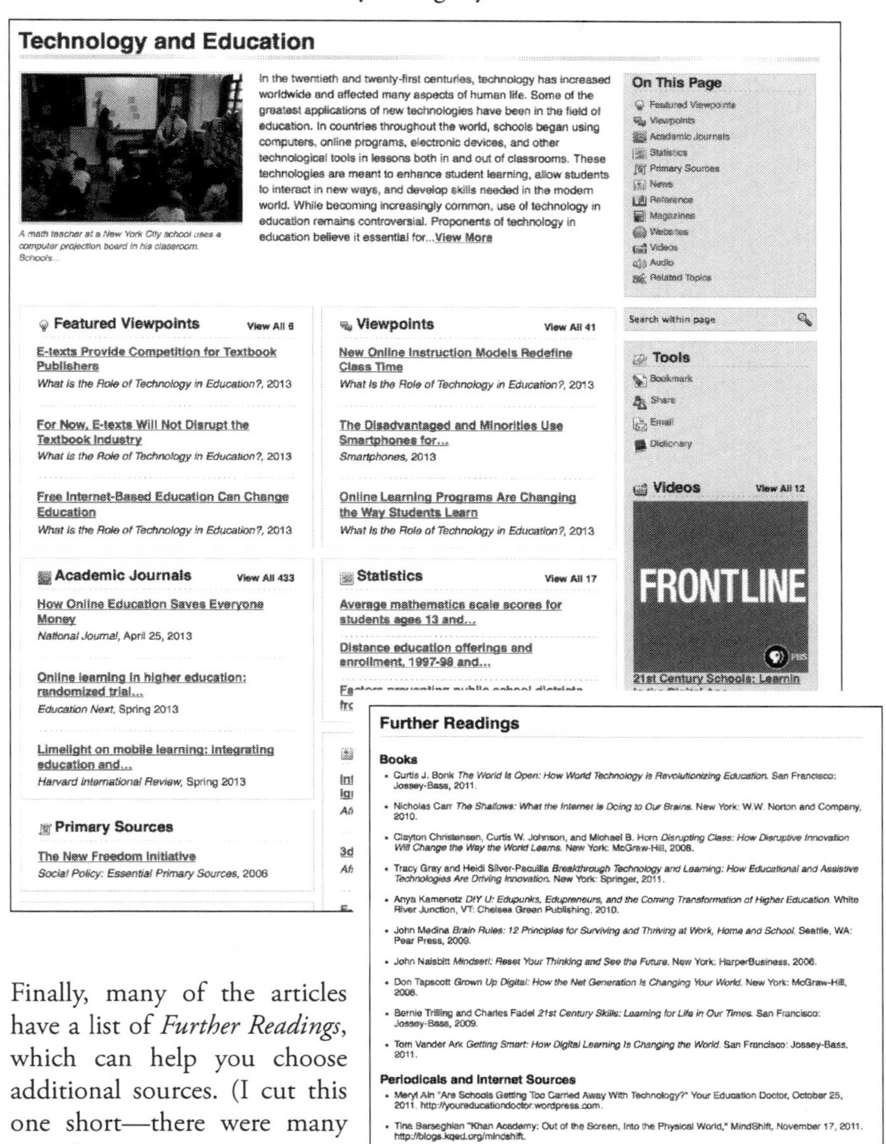

Further Readings

Books

- Curtis J. Bonk *The World Is Open: How World Technology Is Revolutionizing Education*. San Francisco: Jossey-Bass, 2011.
- Nicholas Carr *The Shallows: What the Internet Is Doing to Our Brains*. New York: W.W. Norton and Company, 2010.
- Clayton Christensen, Curtis W. Johnson, and Michael B. Horn *Disrupting Class: How Disruptive Innovation Will Change the Way the World Learns*. New York: McGraw-Hill, 2008.
- Tracy Gray and Heidi Silver-Pacuilla *Breakthrough Technology and Learning: How Educational and Assistive Technologies Are Driving Innovation*. New York: Springer, 2011.
- Anya Kamenetz *DIY U: Edupunks, Edupreneurs, and the Coming Transformation of Higher Education*. White River Junction, VT: Chelsea Green Publishing, 2010.
- John Medina *Brain Rules: 12 Principles for Surviving and Thriving at Work, Home and School*. Seattle, WA: Pear Press, 2009.
- John Naisbitt *Mindset!: Reset Your Thinking and See the Future*. New York: HarperBusiness, 2006.
- Don Tapscott *Grown Up Digital: How the Net Generation Is Changing Your World*. New York: McGraw-Hill, 2008.
- Bernie Trilling and Charles Fadel *21st Century Skills: Learning for Life in Our Times*. San Francisco: Jossey-Bass, 2009.
- Tom Vander Ark *Getting Smart: How Digital Learning Is Changing the World*. San Francisco: Jossey-Bass, 2011.

Periodicals and Internet Sources

- Meryl Ain "Are Schools Getting Too Carried Away With Technology?" Your Education Doctor, October 25, 2011. http://youreducationdoctor.wordpress.com.
- Tina Barseghian "Khan Academy: Out of the Screen, Into the Physical World," MindShift, November 17, 2011. http://blogs.kqed.org/mindshift.
- Nicholas Carr "The Web Shatters Focus, Rewires Brains," *Wired*, May 24, 2011.

Finally, many of the articles have a list of *Further Readings*, which can help you choose additional sources. (I cut this one short—there were many more.)

CHOOSING THE RIGHT DATABASE

General Interest, Not Exclusively Scholarly	
General OneFile **MasterFILE Premier**	These databases have many articles from general interest, nonacademic magazines such as *Time*, *Newsweek*, *U.S. News & World Report*, etc., dating back to 1980 (1975 for MasterFile).
CQ Researcher **Opposing Viewpoints in Context** **Issues and Controversies**	Here you'll find up-to-date information on a broad range of recent issues. These databases are useful if you're writing a persuasive or argumentative essay on a topic of current interest such as affirmative action, salary caps for professional sports, gay rights, and so on. Start here if you're trying to choose a topic for an argumentative paper.
LexisNexis (newspapers) **Newspaper Source** ***New York Times* Historical**	These databases give you access to back issues of many daily newspapers from across the country and around the world. There are also more localized newspaper databases available; here in Massachusetts, for example, we have a database devoted specifically to the *Boston Globe*, the *Boston Herald*, and a number of smaller, local papers.
More specialized, more scholarly	
Academic OneFile **Academic Search Premier** **ProQuest Research Library**	These databases have a good mix of general-interest articles from popular magazines, but they also have the academic journals that you'll need for more advanced writing assignments. If your professor requires sources from "peer-reviewed" journals, this is where you should be looking.
Specialized databases (by field)	

Check your library's holdings. Most subscribe to specialized databases in nursing, business, literature, law, and many other fields.

chapter 10

MLA DOCUMENTATION

I am disillusioned enough to know that no man's opinion on any subject is worth a damn unless backed up with enough genuine information to make him really know what he's talking about.

~ H. P. Lovecraft

Why do your teachers care so much about documentation?

If you understand why documentation is important to academic work, you're more likely to do it accurately in your papers—and avoid a charge of plagiarism. Documenting your sources serves two purposes. First, it allows readers to know which information or ideas belong to you and which are the product of your research. Second, it enables readers to find those sources and examine them on their own.

When do you need to document?

You need to document your source any time you use an idea or piece of information that is not yours. If you don't document your sources properly, you may be accused of plagiarism (see end of Chapter 6).

When do you *not* need to document?

You don't need to cite "common knowledge," which includes strictly factual information that can be found in a number of different sources. For example, if you were writing a paper about Ireland and wanted to mention that the famine happened between 1845 and 1850, you wouldn't need to document that fact since it's widely available as a "fact" and not disputed. On the other hand, let's say that you read an article in which the researcher asserted that the famine did not affect Ireland's Blasket Islands because the Islanders had a diet that was less reliant on potatoes. You *would* need to document this because the idea/assertion is not purely factual. The key difference is that the assertion about the Blasket Islanders is open to dispute or different interpretations. Anything that can be disputed or interpreted needs to be documented.

MLA, APA, Chicago, etc.—which one do you use?

It depends on what kind of paper you're writing because researchers in different fields follow different rules.

In English, for example, you use MLA (Modern Language Association), which is what this chapter covers. In psychology and other social sciences, you use APA (American Psychological Association), covered in Chapter 11. In history and other fields, it's Chicago. For most of the sciences, it's CSE (Council of Science Editors).

All four systems have some common features, so learning MLA should help you adapt to those other documentation styles.

MLA Documentation: a two-part process

Documenting your sources properly is a two-step process. Within your paper, you provide a brief reference to your source; this is called an in-text citation. At the end of the paper you provide complete information for all of your sources—this is the works-cited page.

MLA Documentation Directory

IN-TEXT CITATIONS

When I say "in-text," I mean *your* text, the essay you're writing. For the examples here, pretend that these are sentences you would write in your paper. Pay attention to punctuation, spacing, and formatting.

BASIC RULES

I'll use a recent article from *The Atlantic* about robotics in medicine for the first few examples. Note that I found this article online (theatlantic.com), though I will also go over how it will look if you use the actual print version of the magazine.

Here's one part of the article that I want to use in my paper:

> Health care already represents one-sixth of America's gross domestic product. And that share is growing, placing an ever-larger strain on paychecks, corporate profits, and government resources. Figuring out how to manage this cost growth—how to meet the aging population's medical needs without bankrupting the country—has become the central economic-policy challenge of our time.

First, I put one of the ideas in my own words (see *paraphrasing* in Chapter 6):

> **Rising health care costs create a potential crisis for the American economy.**

But this isn't my idea. *I* didn't come to this conclusion based on my research. The author of the article, Jonathan Cohn, did.

Important: No matter how you identify the "source" (usually the author), it must correspond with a works-cited entry In other words, you must have a works-cited entry that begins **Cohn, Jonathan.**

There are two ways to give Cohn credit:

Method #1: Name the source in the sentence

This is the preferred method for citing a source. Use Jonathan Cohn's name in a signal phrase (again, see Chapter 6).

> **Jonathan Cohn argues that rising health care costs create a potential crisis for the American economy.**

Note: You only write the author's full name the first time you refer to him. After that, it would just be the last name: "Cohn argues that robots. . . ."

Method #2: Don't name the source in the sentence

If you don't name the source in your sentence via a signal phrase, you must do so in the parenthetical reference at the end of the sentence. Many professors prefer that students avoid this citation method; check with your professor.

> **Rising health care costs create a potential crisis for the American economy (Cohn).**

Using quotations

The two methods above work the same using a *direct quotation* (the writer's exact words, in his or her order):

> **Cohn observes that rising health care costs are "the central economic-policy challenge of our time."**

Or:

> **One commentator believes that rising health care costs are "the central economic-policy challenge of our time" (Cohn).**

Note how the end of the sentence works; the order of these elements is important. First, close the quotes, and then type a space, then the parentheses for the citation information, then the period.

Using a source in print (an actual book, magazine, etc.)

If you're holding a physical publication in your hand, you should include page numbers in your citation. I happen to subscribe to *The Atlantic*, and I also read this article in the magazine; the information I've been citing appeared on page 61, so my citations (all four versions of what you saw on the previous page) would like this:

> **Jonathan Cohn argues that rising health care costs create a potential crisis for the American economy (61).**

> **Rising health care costs create a potential crisis for the American economy (Cohn 61).**

Cohn observes that rising health care costs are "the central economic-policy challenge of our time" (61).

One commentator believes that rising health care costs are "the central economic-policy challenge of our time" (Cohn 61).

Note: There's no comma between the last name and the page number.

Changing the wording of quotations

Generally, you should quote your sources precisely, using their exact words. But sometimes you'll need to change a word or two for grammatical purposes, or remove part of a quotation. Let's say that I want to quote part of this sentence:

> The idea of robots performing surgery or more-routine medical tasks with less supervision is something many experts take seriously.

Just for the sake of this example, let's say that I want to restructure the quoted portion of the sentence, like this:

Cohn notes that if "robots [perform] surgery or more-routine medical tasks with less supervision," new concerns will arise.

Because I'm no longer quoting Cohn word for word (*performing* has become *perform*), I have to indicate the alteration of the original wording by putting the word I've changed inside brackets.

Integrating material into your sentences

Notice that in all of my sample sentences I have *integrated* the quoted or paraphrased material into my sentences. Make the material that you refer to *a part of* your sentence, and make sure that your sentence reads smoothly and is grammatically correct. Refer to Chapter 6 for additional guidelines.

COMPLICATIONS TO THE BASIC RULES

Generally, the above examples will get you through the vast majority of in-text citations. But there's a good chance you'll have to deal with some variations.

No author listed

Pretend that the article in *The Atlantic* did not have an author listed; in that case, use a shortened form (if it needs to be shortened) of the title of the article, inside quotation marks:

> **One commentator believes that rising health care costs are "the central economic-policy challenge of our time" ("The Robot Will See You Now").**
>
> *if you read it in print:* **of our time" ("The Robot Will See You Now" 61).**

Note: How you abbreviate the title is up to you, but be sure to use the first word—because this is the word a reader would be looking for on the works-cited page.

Two or three authors

For the sake of simplicity, let's pretend that the article in *The Atlantic* was written by two or three authors. First, let's add a second author, James Gillen:

> **Cohn and Gillen argue that rising health care costs create a potential crisis for the American economy.**

Or:

> **Rising health care costs create a potential crisis for the American economy (Cohn and Gillen).**

If there had been a third author (let's pretend she's named Delia Morlund), and she were listed third, your parenthetical citation would look like this:

> **Cohn, Gillen, and Morlund argue that rising health care costs create a potential crisis for the American economy.**

Or:

> **Rising health care costs create a potential crisis for the American economy (Cohn, Gillen, and Morlund).**

Page numbers: Remember that if you read this article in print, you would need to add page numbers to the citations; follow guidelines on pages 132-133.

Four or more authors

Let's further assume that the above example added a fourth author, Seth Jackson. If you name the authors in your sentence, you use the first author's name only, followed by *et al.*, which is Latin for *and others*.

> **Jonathan Cohn et al. argue that rising health care costs create a potential crisis for the American economy.**

Or, if you don't want to name the authors in the sentence:

> **Rising health care costs create a potential crisis for the American economy (Cohn et al.).**

Page numbers: Remember that if you read this article in print, you would need to add page numbers to the citations; follow guidelines on pages 132-133.

Quoting someone who's being quoted

Yes, this is tricky—but not all that uncommon. In this example, I want to use part of the following quote, from the same article in *The Atlantic*.

> "We do now have robots performing surgery, but the robot is under constant supervision of the surgeon during the process," Baumol told a reporter from *The New York Times* two years ago. "You haven't saved labor. You have done other good things, but it isn't a way of cheapening the process."

Remember two things, and you'll get it right.

First, mention the person you're quoting (Baumol, in this case) in your sentence, and use his or her full name—which I had to find earlier in the article. Then, in your parenthetical reference, use the abbreviation *qtd. in* (for "quoted in") before the author of the article—because that's what your reader will be looking for on the works-cited page if she wants to find the article.

> **Economist William Baumol notes that the robots are "under constant supervision of the surgeon during the process" (qtd. in Cohn).**

Print version: If you read this in the print version of the magazine, your citation would be:

> **Economist William Baumol notes that the robots are "under constant supervision of the surgeon during the process" (qtd. in Cohn 66).**

Long quotation (also known as block quotation)

If you quote something that is four lines or longer, format it as follows (see page 138 for word processing directions); always mention the author's name in your sentence that preceeds the block quotation.

Your writing, to introduce the quotation.

By examining the marketing practices of mainstream grocery stores, Pollan reveals the preeminence of quantification:

Block quotation, indented 1 inch from left. The right margin stays the same. It's double-spaced just like the rest of your text.

> **Just look at the typical newspaper ad for a supermarket. The sole quality on display here is actually a quantity: tomatoes $0.69 a pound; ground chuck $1.09 a pound; eggs $0.99 a dozen—special this week. Is there any other category of product sold on such a reductive basis? (136)**

Your writing, to comment on the quotation.

By highlighting the focus on price and quantity, Pollan exposes a peculiar—and potentially dangerous—complicity between consumers and grocery businesses.

Also note that the block quotation ends with the page number where you found the quotation, inside parentheses and *after* the punctuation mark. If your source has no page number, don't bother with the parenthetical reference.

Work in an anthology

An anthology is a collection of essays, stories, or poems by many different authors. Many textbooks used in English courses are anthologies. For the in-text citation, you don't really need to worry about the fact that the book is an anthology. Just be sure that your citation refers to the actual writer of the story, poem or essay—not the editor(s) of the anthology.

> **Jane Smiley suggests that the problem may have its source in "the ubiquity of sugar" (328).**

Or:

> **Perhaps the problem is "the ubiquity of sugar" (Smiley 328).**

When you do the works-cited entry, you'll need to know the name of Smiley's essay, "Reflections on a Lettuce Wedge," the name of the anthology it appeared in, the name(s) of the anthology's editor(s), and other publication information. See page 148 for more information.

Organization or group as author

It's best to name the organization in your sentence:

> **According to the Modern Language Association, "The study of the most popular languages—Spanish, French, and German—continues to grow and represents more than 70 percent of language enrollments."**

But you can also do it the other way:

> **Recent research suggests that students continue to study the most traditionally popular languages; more than 70 percent of students are taking Spanish, French, and German (Modern Language Association).**

Note: I did not include a page number for either citation because I found the quotation on the organization's website.

Author who wrote two or more books (that you cite in your paper)

Let's say that I read two books by Michael Pollan (*The Omnivore's Dilemma* and *In Defense of Food*), and I'm using them both as sources in my paper. So that there's no confusion about which book I'm referring to, I need to provide a shortened reference to the book inside the parentheses.

> **Michael Pollan asserts that both our civilization and our "food system" are "strictly organized on industrial lines" (*Omnivore* 201).**

Or:

> **It has been argued that both our civilization and our "food system" are "strictly organized on industrial lines" (Pollan, *Omnivore* 201).**

Note: If I had been using an article rather than a book, I would have still used a shortened form of the title, but it would be inside quotation marks, not italicized.

Two authors with same last name

It doesn't happen very often, but it does happen. If you refer to the author within the sentence, use the first and last name each time.

> **Christopher Alexander describes the problem this way: "A complex of buildings with no center is like a man without a head" (486).**

Or:

> **One architectural theorist describes the problem this way: "A complex of buildings with no center is like a man without a head" (C. Alexander 486).**

Formatting a Block Quotation

TIP: WORD PROCESSING

If you quote something four or more lines long, format it as follows.

1. Start by highlighting the text you're quoting. Then, click on the **View** tab.

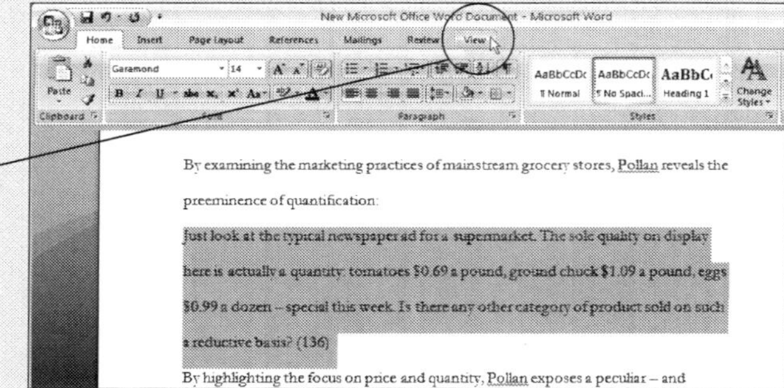

2. Check the **Ruler** box.

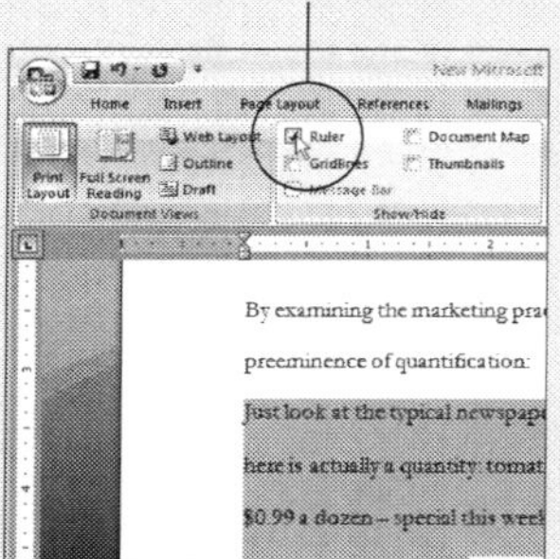

3. This little gadget is made up of three parts. You want to click on and hold the bottom one, the very small square, then drag it 1/2 inch to the right.

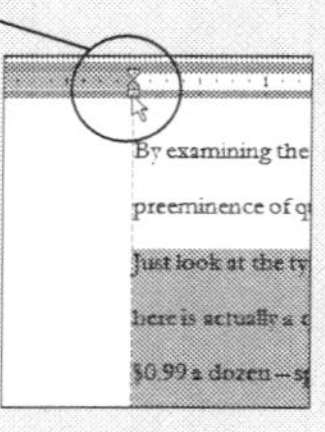

4. This is how it should look when you're finished.

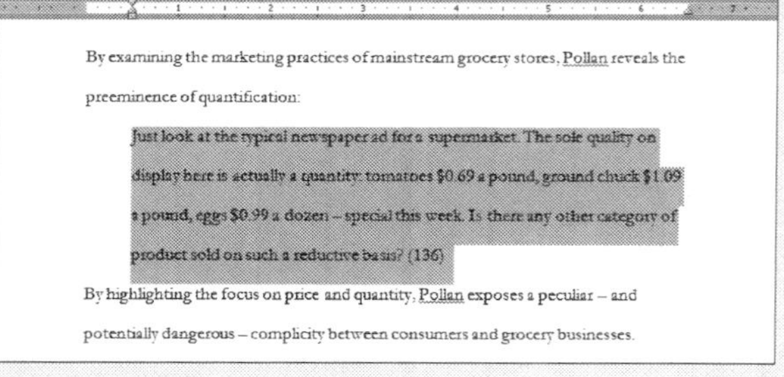

Two or more authors in the same sentence

Put the parenthetical citation immediately after the information you're citing from each author.

> **It has been said that heightened awareness of the sources of our food connects people to their "agricultural roots" (Smiley 437), or even to their "feral past" (Winckler 28).**

Two authors who make the same point

Again, this will happen only rarely. Your citation should name both authors, separated by a semi-colon.

> **(Pollan 486; Jones 54).**

Citing a Kindle, Nook, or other e-reader

Provide more information than you usually would (at least until the makers of e-readers and the MLA come to some agreement); many scholars are including some reference to the chapter in which source material appeared:

> **In Chapter 10, "Grass," Michael Pollan asserts that both our civilization and our "food system" are "strictly organized on industrial lines."**

Radio broadcast / podcast

See pages 158-159 for complete illustration of both in-text citation guidelines and works-cited information.

WORKS-CITED ENTRIES

FIRST, A FEW UNIVERSAL GUIDELINES

The information on the next two pages is essential—don't skip past it. You will likely need to come back to these basic guidelines as you write your works-cited entries.

Capitalization

I admit it—it doesn't make much sense that you're supposed to capitalize titles "properly" when the journal or magazine article you're citing hasn't done so. I'm not sure why this happens, but all you really need to know is that it's your job to do it right whether your source does or not.

Always capitalize	the first and last words of the title
	nouns, verbs, adjectives, and adverbs
Do *not* capitalize	prepositions: of, on, around, behind, and many more
	articles: a, an, the
	conjunctions: and, but, or, for, nor, so, yet
	infinitive: to

So, even though a *Sports Illustrated* article looks like this (Over The Top) in the database, you would write, Over the Top.

Long titles

Sometimes, particularly with newspaper and magazine articles, you'll come across some very long titles. Or at least they look that way; in many cases, what you're seeing is a headline and a sub-headline.

You have to use your judgment about what's really the title and what's not, but I do have a few suggestions. Use the whole title, even if it's long, when it's the title of a book or an article in a scholarly journal. Use a shortened version of the title when it's very, very long and/or the second part appears to be a complete sentence. Whenever possible, it helps to look at the original (or a PDF) so you can see the original formatting—then it's often obvious what the *real* title is.

Author names

The basic rule is that you reverse the order of the first author's name, but leave the others in usual order.

One author: Smith, Doug K.

If Smith didn't have a middle initial: Smith, Doug.

Two authors: Smith, Doug K., and Walter T. White.

If Smith didn't have a middle initial: Smith, Doug, and Walter T. White.

Three authors: Smith, Doug K., Walter T. White, and Bertha Q. McBride.

If Smith didn't have a middle initial:

Smith, Doug, Walter T. White, and Bertha Q. McBride.

Four authors: Smith, Doug K., et al. (Et al. is an abbreviation for *and others.*)

If Smith didn't have a middle initial: Smith, Doug, et al.

Abbreviations of months

Most months are abbreviated; here's how all of them should look:

Jan.	**Feb.**	**Mar.**	**Apr.**	**May**	**June**
July	**Aug.**	**Sept.**	**Oct.**	**Nov.**	**Dec.**

Abbreviations of publishers' names

If the publisher is listed as, for example, The Macmillan Company, you would simply write Macmillan.

For academic journals, their publisher is often a university press. If, for example, it's Harvard University Press, you would abbreviate it Harvard UP (no period—but my sentence now needs one).

Spaces

With some of the examples on the following pages, it's hard to tell where you should have a space. You always have a space after any mark of punctuation (comma, period, colon, semi-colon); also rememember that between each "part" of an entry (like, for example, between a magazine name and its date of publication), you always need a space.

Sample works-cited page

To see a properly formatted works-cited page, look at the sample student essay by Kyle Wright on pages 44-45.

HOW THE REST OF THIS CHAPTER IS ORGANIZED

The rest of this chapter is organized as follows:

- Books (pages 142 – 149)
- Articles from the Internet and databases (pages 149 – 159)
- Other sources (pages 160 – 162)
- Articles from print sources (pages 163 – 164)

Note: Because this book is intended to be a quick guide to the most common issues facing first-year writers, there are some sources that I'm not including here. If there's something I don't cover that you need to know how to cite, I highly recommend the Purdue University site, *The Owl at Purdue*. Do a Google search for *Purdue Owl MLA* to find it.

BOOKS

Book with one author

Author's Last Name, First Name. *Book Title: Book Subtitle. City of Publication: Publisher, Year of Publication. Medium.**

* Include subtitle after a colon, and always capitalize the first word after the colon.

Pollan, Michael. *The Omnivore's Dilemma: A Natural History of Four Meals*. New York: Penguin, 2006. Print.

Hanging indent

One of the unusual characteristics of the works-cited page is the "hanging indent." We do it this way because the Modern Language Association tells us to, but also because it makes sense. When you have quite a few works-cited entries, it's easier for the reader to find a particular source by browsing down the left side of the page to find the author name. You're much better off learning how to do it as I show on the next page rather than using your tab key, which almost always results in weird formatting that's hard to fix.

TIP: WORD PROCESSING

Formatting a Hanging Indent

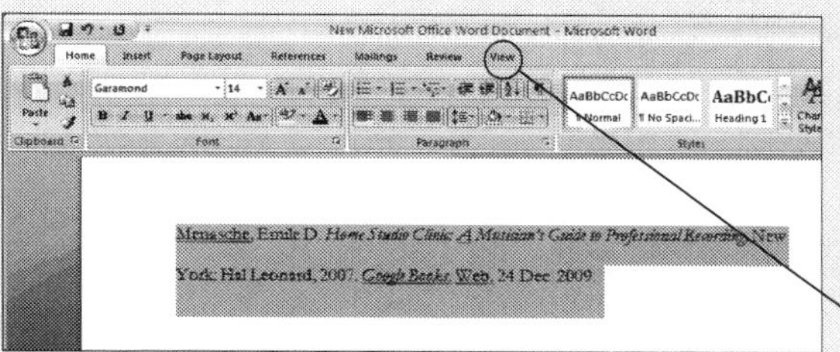

1. Start by highlighting all of your works cited entries. (It's best to do this when you're finished typing all the entries—I'm only doing one here.) Then, click on the **View** tab.

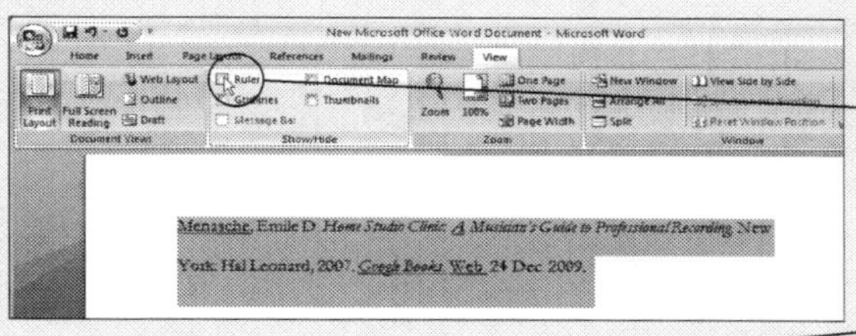

2. Check the **Ruler** box.

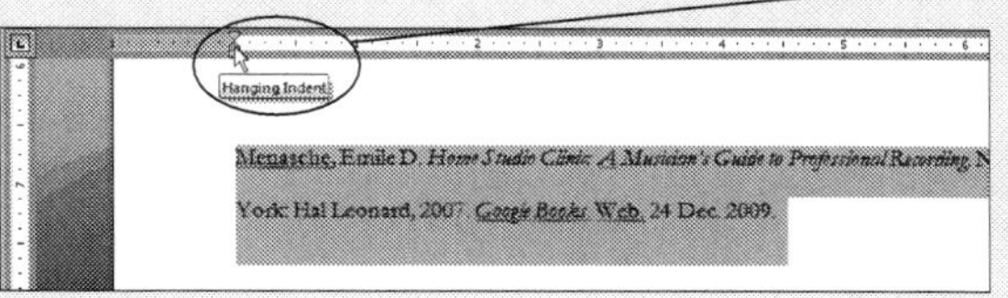

3. This little gadget is made up of three parts. You want to click on and hold the triangular one in the middle, then drag it 1/2 inch to the right.

Note: If you let your cursor hover over the boxes, it will display the function; when it says **Hanging Indent**, you've got the right one.

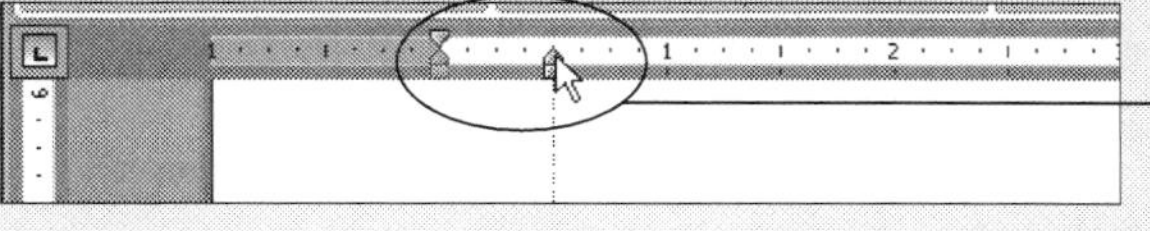

5. After dragging that triangular piece to the right, this is how it should look.

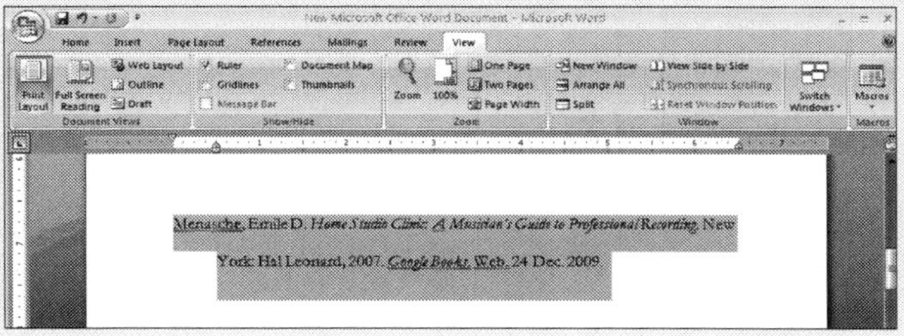

6. Done.

The front cover

Here you should find the full title, though sometimes there's so much additional information on the cover that it can be hard to tell exactly what the title is. When there's a subtitle, it's even more confusing. Looking at the title page can help.

The title page

Title, subtitle, author and publisher—all on one page. (It's not always this straightforward.)

Note: Everything here is capitalized, which you do not want to do in your documentation. See specific guidelines on capitalization on page 140.

The spine

The spine (or edge) of the book will usually have the full name of the book (often with subtitle, as in this case) and the author's full name. The spine is also the most reliable place to find the name of the publisher; this case is unusual in that it shows a penguin rather than the name of the publisher, which happens to be . . . Penguin Books.

The copyright page

You will need to look at this page, usually, to find out what year the book was published and what city the publisher is in. This is unfortunate, because there's so much information on this page that it can be difficult to find what you need.

If you look at all the cities listed here, you could easily get confused about the city of publication. It's almost always the first one listed: New York, in this case.

PENGUIN BOOKS
Published by the Penguin Group
Penguin Group (USA) Inc., 375 Hudson Street, New York, New York 10014, U.S.A.
Penguin Group (Canada), 90 Eglinton Avenue East, Suite 700, Toronto,
Ontario, Canada M4P 2Y3 (a division of Pearson Penguin Canada Inc.)
Penguin Books Ltd, 80 Strand, London WC2R 0RL, England
Penguin Ireland, 25 St Stephen's Green, Dublin 2, Ireland (a division of Penguin Books Ltd)
Penguin Group (Australia), 250 Camberwell Road, Camberwell,
Victoria 3124, Australia (a division of Pearson Australia Group Pty Ltd)
Penguin Books India Pvt Ltd, 11 Community Centre, Panchsheel Park, New Delhi – 110 017, Ir
Penguin Group (NZ), 67 Apollo Drive, Rosedale, North Shore 0745,
Auckland, New Zealand (a division of Pearson New Zealand Ltd)
Penguin Books (South Africa) (Pty) Ltd, 24 Sturdee Avenue,
Rosebank, Johannesburg 2196, South Africa

Penguin Books Ltd, Registered Offices:
80 Strand, London WC2R 0RL, England

First published in the United States of America by The Penguin Press,
a member of Penguin Group (USA) Inc. 2006
Published in Penguin Books 2007

3 5 7 9 10 8 6 4 2

Copyright © Michael Pollan, 2006
All rights reserved

The year of publication appears after the © symbol, in this case, 2006.

THE LIBRARY OF CONGRESS HAS CATALOGED THE HARDCOVER EDITION AS FOLLOWS:
Pollan, Michael.
The omnivore's dilemma : a natural history of four meals / Michael Pollan.
p. cm.
Includes bibliographical references and index.
ISBN 1-59420-082-3 (hc.)
ISBN 978-0-14-303858-0 (pbk.)
1. GT2850.P65 2006. 2. Food habits. 3. Food preferences. I. Title.
GT2850.P65 2006
394.1'2—dc22 2005056557

Printed in the United States of America
DESIGNED BY MARYSARAH QUINN

Book with two, three, four or more authors

See guidelines on page 141 for how to write additional author names.

Book with an editor

The editor is listed as the "main" author for the sake of the works-cited entry. Keep in mind, though, that if you cite particular essays or stories from within this book, you need an entry for each of these authors too. Yes, this is a little confusing. See also the guideline for *Work in an anthology* on page 148.

As far as the works-cited entry goes, this is just like any other book, with the simple addition of the abbreviation *eds.* for the editors. If there had been only one editor, the abbreviation would be *ed.* (not italicized in either case).

> Hofstadter, Albert, and Richard Kuhns, eds. *Philosophies of Art and Beauty: Selected Readings in Aesthetics from Plato to Heidegger.* Chicago: University of Chicago Press, 1964. Print.

Book that lists an edition

Many books (textbooks, especially) are republished with the same title but new content. If your book has an edition listed, it will probably be noticeable on the cover and/or the spine. In the works-cited entry, put the edition after the title.

> McQuade, Donald, and Robert Atwan, eds. *The Writer's Presence: A Pool of Readings*. 5th ed. Boston: Bedford / St. Martin's, 2007. Print.

Two or more books by same author

Use three hyphens to indicate a repeat of the author's name. Put each book in alphabetical order (*In* before *Omnivore*).

> Pollan, Michael. *In Defense of Food: An Eater's Manifesto*. New York: Penguin, 2008. Print.

> ---. *The Omnivore's Dilemma: A Natural History of Four Meals*. New York: Penguin, 2006. Print.

Book by an anonymous author

Don't write Anonymous or Anon. for the author. Just go straight to the title.

Primary Colors: A Novel of Politics. New York: Random House, 2006. Print.

Book by an organization or group

Start with the name of the organization or group, followed by the book title.

Modern Language Association. *MLA Style Manual and Guide to Scholarly Publishing*. 3rd ed. New York: Modern Language Association of America, 2008. Print.

Book that has been translated

Start with the person who wrote the book, *not* the translator.

Barthes, Roland. *The Eiffel Tower and Other Mythologies*. Trans. Richard Howard. New York: Noonday, 1979. Print.

Book in more than one volume

After the title, write the volume number that you used; after the year of publication, write the total number of volumes of the book.

Kelby, Scott. *The Digital Photography Book*. Vol. 2. Berkeley: Peachpit Press, 2008. 2 vols. Print.

Book that has a title within the title

When scholars write about another book, they often include the title of the book in *their* title. Don't italicize the title that appears within their title.

Brodhead, Richard H., ed. *New Essays on* Moby-Dick. Cambride, Mass.: Cambride UP, 1986. Print.

Work in an anthology—a book with many different authors

Many textbooks, particularly in English classes, are *anthologies*; an anthology is a collection of works (essays, stories, poems, and/or plays) written by many different authors. If you're using one essay from an anthology here's how you cite it:

Author's Last Name, First Name. "Title of Essay." *Name of Book*. Ed. First Name Last Name. City of Publication: Publisher, Year of Publication. Page range. Medium.

Hughes, Langston. "Salvation." *The Writer's Presence: A Pool of Readings*. Eds. Donald McQuade and Robert Atwan. Boston: Bedford / St. Martin's, 2007. 163-65. Print.

- This is the guideline for when you're citing only one essay, story, play, or poem from an anthology; if you cite more than one, see the next entry.
- Use Ed. for one editor, Eds. for two or more. The editors' names will be on the front of the book and on the title page.

Two or more works from the same anthology

When you use two different authors from the same anthology, you have to do the works-cited entries very differently. Do a shortened entry for each essay, story, or poem, and also do a full entry for the whole book.

Note: Put each entry on your works-cited page wherever it belongs alphabetically; in other words, these would not necessarily be grouped together.

Entry for individual essay you read in the anthology

Hughes, Langston. "Salvation." McQuade and Atwan 163-65.

Full entry for whole book

McQuade, Donald, and Robert Atwan, eds. 5th ed. *The Writer's Presence: A Pool of Readings*. Boston: Bedford / St. Martin's, 2007. Print.

Entry for individual essay you read in the anthology

Wolfe, Tom. "Hooking Up." McQuade and Atwan 611-18.

Encyclopedia or dictionary

In most reference books (such as encyclopedias and dictionaries), no author is listed, so you simply start with the title of the entry. After the name of the book, include the edition (abbreviated as below) and the year. If there *is* an author listed, then put that first. But I have a feeling you knew that.

"Botox." *The New Encyclopædia Britannica.* 15th ed. 2003. Print.

Book that you read online

Author's Last Name, First Name. *Book Title: Book Subtitle.* City of Publication: Publisher, Year of Publication. *Name of Site.* Medium. Date of access.

Menasche, Emile D. *Home Studio Clinic: A Musician's Guide to Professional Recording.* New York: Hal Leonard, 2007. *Google Books.* Web. 24 Dec. 2009.

- Abbreviate months as shown on page 141.
- For two, three, four or more authors, see page 141.

ARTICLES FROM THE INTERNET AND DATABASES

For many of you, this is where you'll find most of your sources, which is why I'm illustrating these guidelines more prominently, with an entire page devoted to six of the most common citations:

- Article (not from an academic journal) you found online
- Article (not from an academic journal) you found in a database
- Article from an academic journal you found online
- Article from an academic journal you found in a database
- Online page published by government agency or other organization/group

Article (not from an academic journal) you found online

This is the guideline you'd use for just about any "article" you find online. It doesn't matter if the publication has a print version or not. Use this guideline for articles from all online magazines and newspapers.

Author's Last Name, First Name. "Title of Article: Subtitle." *Name of Website.* Publisher, Date. Medium. Date of access.

Cohn, Jonathan. "The Robot Will See You Now." *The Atlantic.* The Atlantic Monthly Group, 20 Feb. 2013. Web. 5 June 2013.

- As in this example, many print magazines also have an online version of the magazine. For the name of the website, use your judgment; in this case, it's clearly *The Atlantic*. Generally, you write the name without *.com*: *Slate, Salon, Time, Newsweek*, etc.
- Generally, you should not include subtitles for magazine articles (see guidelines for long titles on page 140).
- Abbreviate months as shown on page 141.
- If the article has no author listed, simply start your entry with the title of the article (inside quotation marks).

Article (not from an academic journal) you found in a database

This isn't very different from the guideline for an online article on the previous page. Here, you omit the publisher information but include the name of the database and the page range. Note also that there's no period after magazine title.

> Author's Last Name, First Name. "Title of Article: Subtitle." *Name of Magazine or Newspaper* Date: page range. *Name of Database.* Medium. Date of access.

> Cohn, Jonathan. "The Robot Will See You Now." *The Atlantic* Mar. 2013: 58+. *Academic OneFile.* Web. 7 June 2013.

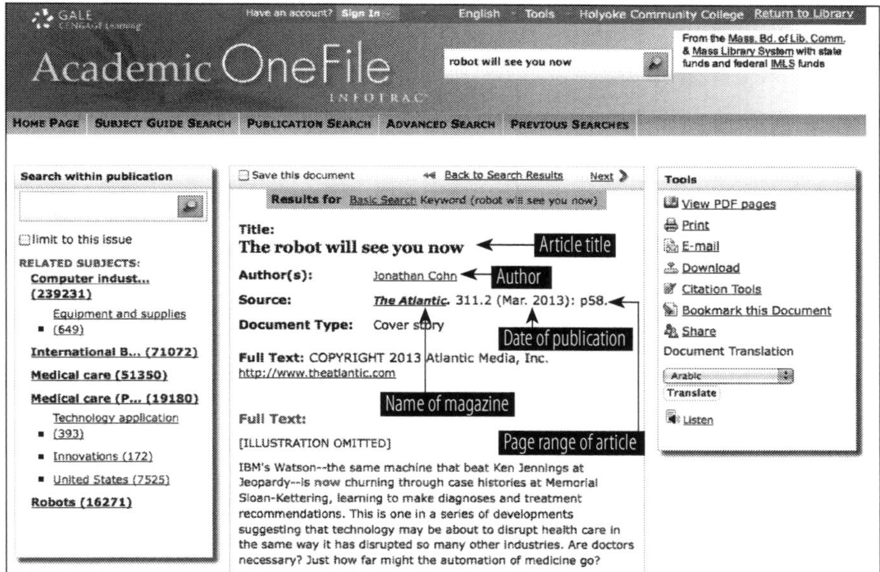

- Note that the guideline calls for a "page range," but the database doesn't provide this information—it only gives the starting page. In this case, use that page and the + symbol, so it looks like this: 58+.
- Note that the capitalization shown for the article title needs to be corrected (see guidelines on page 140).
- Generally, you should not include subtitles for magazine articles (see guidelines for long titles on page 140).
- Abbreviate months as shown on page 141.

Article from an academic journal you found online

I found this article while searching Google Scholar.

Author's Last Name, First Name. "Title of Article: Subtitle." *Name of Journal* Volume.Issue (Year): Page range. Medium. Date of access.

Ro, Hyun Kyoung, Patrick T. Terenzini, and Alexander C. Yin. "Between-College Effects on Students Reconsidered." *Research in Higher Education* 54.3 (May 2013): 253-282. Web. 5 June 2013.

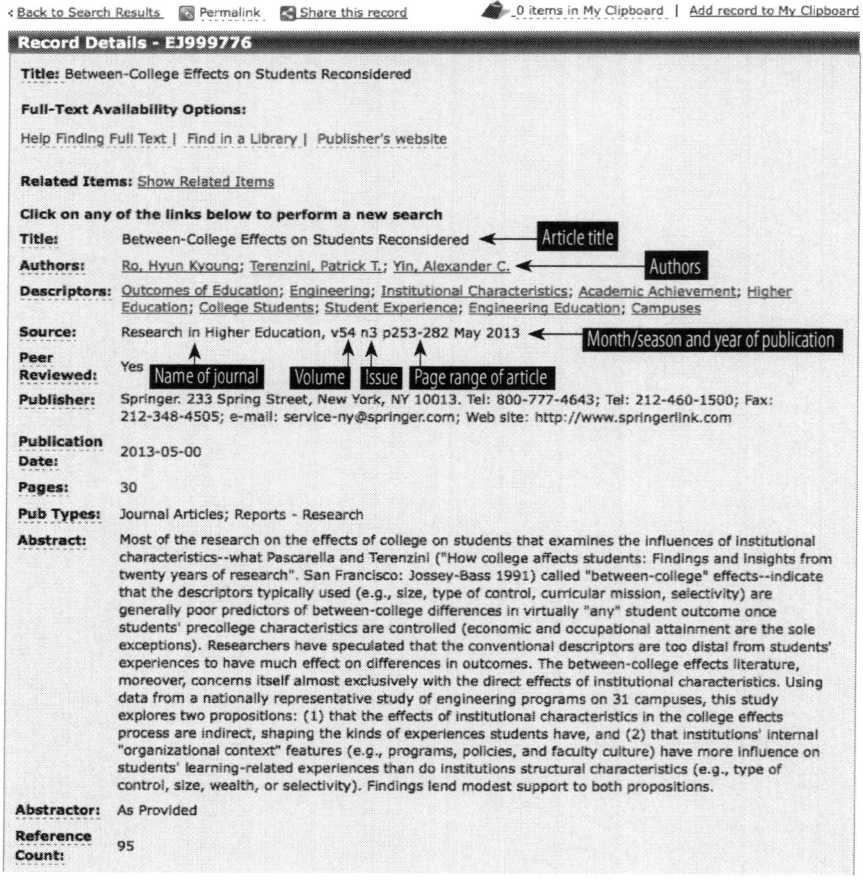

‹ Back to Search Results | Permalink | Share this record | 0 items in My Clipboard | Add record to My Clipboard

Record Details - EJ999776

Title: Between-College Effects on Students Reconsidered

Full-Text Availability Options:

Help Finding Full Text | Find in a Library | Publisher's website

Related Items: Show Related Items

Click on any of the links below to perform a new search

Title: Between-College Effects on Students Reconsidered

Authors: Ro, Hyun Kyoung; Terenzini, Patrick T.; Yin, Alexander C.

Descriptors: Outcomes of Education; Engineering; Institutional Characteristics; Academic Achievement; Higher Education; College Students; Student Experience; Engineering Education; Campuses

Source: Research in Higher Education, v54 n3 p253-282 May 2013

Peer Reviewed: Yes

Publisher: Springer. 233 Spring Street, New York, NY 10013. Tel: 800-777-4643; Tel: 212-460-1500; Fax: 212-348-4505; e-mail: service-ny@springer.com; Web site: http://www.springerlink.com

Publication Date: 2013-05-00

Pages: 30

Pub Types: Journal Articles; Reports - Research

Abstract: Most of the research on the effects of college on students that examines the influences of institutional characteristics--what Pascarella and Terenzini ("How college affects students: Findings and insights from twenty years of research". San Francisco: Jossey-Bass 1991) called "between-college" effects--indicate that the descriptors typically used (e.g., size, type of control, curricular mission, selectivity) are generally poor predictors of between-college differences in virtually "any" student outcome once students' precollege characteristics are controlled (economic and occupational attainment are the sole exceptions). Researchers have speculated that the conventional descriptors are too distal from students' experiences to have much effect on differences in outcomes. The between-college effects literature, moreover, concerns itself almost exclusively with the direct effects of institutional characteristics. Using data from a nationally representative study of engineering programs on 31 campuses, this study explores two propositions: (1) that the effects of institutional characteristics in the college effects process are indirect, shaping the kinds of experiences students have, and (2) that institutions' internal "organizational context" features (e.g., programs, policies, and faculty culture) have more influence on students' learning-related experiences than do institutions structural characteristics (e.g., type of control, size, wealth, or selectivity). Findings lend modest support to both propositions.

Abstractor: As Provided

Reference Count: 95

Article from an academic journal you found in a database

I found this article in the *Academic Search Premier* database.

Author's Last Name, First Name. "Title of Article." *Name of Journal* Volume. Issue (Year): Page range. *Name of Database*. Medium. Date you accessed article.

Steinberg, Shirley R., and Joe L. Kincheloe. "Privileged and Getting Away with It: The Cultural Studies of White, Middle-Class Youth." *Studies in the Literary Imagination* 31.1 (Spring 1998): 103-27. *Academic Search Premier*. Web. 5 June 2013.

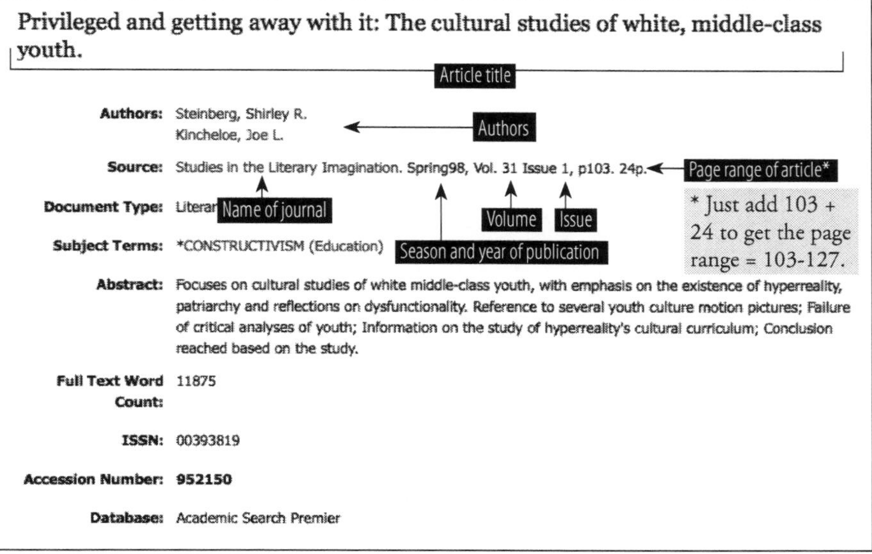

Privileged and getting away with it: The cultural studies of white, middle-class youth.

Authors: Steinberg, Shirley R.; Kincheloe, Joe L.

Source: Studies in the Literary Imagination. Spring98, Vol. 31 Issue 1, p103. 24p.

Document Type: Literar[y]

Subject Terms: *CONSTRUCTIVISM (Education)

Abstract: Focuses on cultural studies of white middle-class youth, with emphasis on the existence of hyperreality, patriarchy and reflections on dysfunctionality. Reference to several youth culture motion pictures; Failure of critical analyses of youth; Information on the study of hyperreality's cultural curriculum; Conclusion reached based on the study.

Full Text Word Count: 11875

ISSN: 00393819

Accession Number: **952150**

Database: Academic Search Premier

- Most articles in academic journals include subtitles, which you should almost always include in your works-cited entry (see guidelines for long titles on page 140).
- There's no punctuation after the name of the journal.
- Format volume and issue numbers correctly, as shown above; often, these look very different in the source itself: Vol. 31, No. 1, or v31n1, etc.
- For three, four, or more authors, see page 141.

Online page published by government agency or other organization / group

This guideline covers most online pages, though you should use a slightly different guideline for government documents (such as census data, etc.); for that, see page

Name of Organization. "Title of Article." *Name of Website*. Publisher, Date. Medium. Date you accessed article.

U.S. Department of Health & Human Services. "Keep Food Safe." *Foodsafety.gov*. U.S. Department of Health & Human Services, 7 June 2013. Web. 7 June 2013.

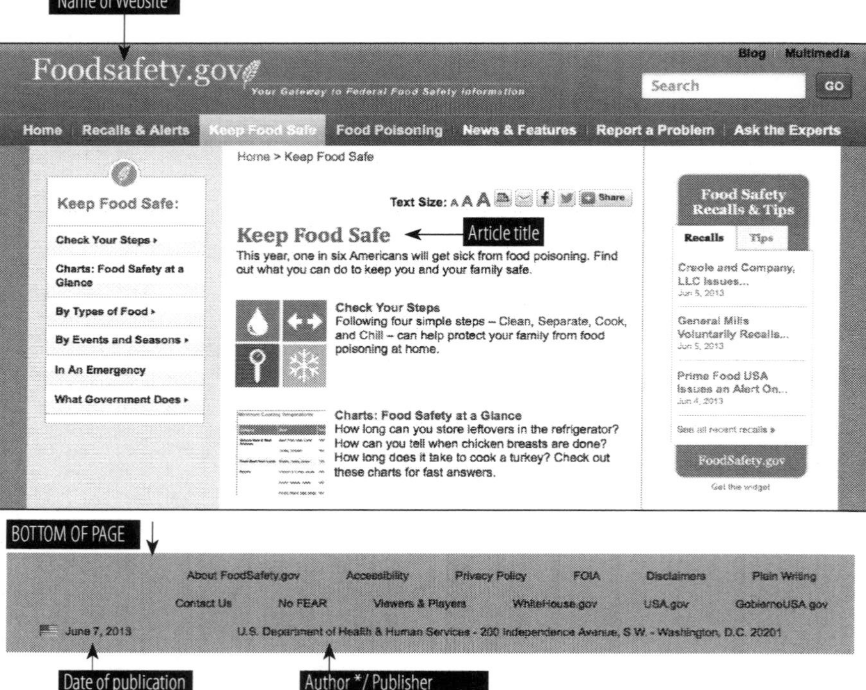

- *Note: This is an unusual circumstance in that the author and the publisher are the same. As in many documentation situations, you have to make a judgment about such things. Also, if there had been a person's name listed as the author, you would obviously use that rather than the organization name.
- Abbreviate months as shown on page 141.

Using a citation generator

TIP: TECHNOLOGY

If you use a library database for research, you'll find that many of the databases offer a "citation generator." This can save you some time if you have a number of database sources, but be sure to check the entries—they often have mistakes.

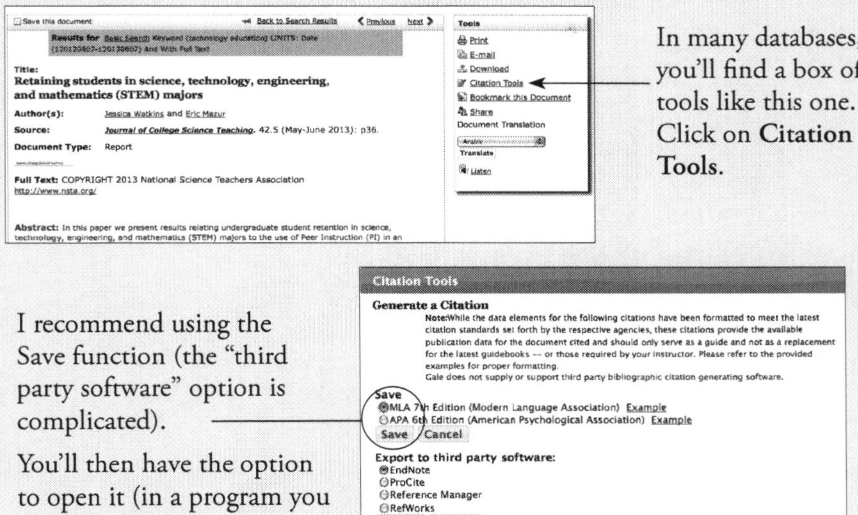

In many databases, you'll find a box of tools like this one. Click on **Citation Tools.**

I recommend using the Save function (the "third party software" option is complicated).

You'll then have the option to open it (in a program you choose) or save it.

If you decide to open it, choose the program you're using to write your paper in (Microsoft Word in this case). This should give you a properly formatted citation; the one below is almost perfect, except for capitalization errors in the article title. The second version below is the corrected (by me) version.

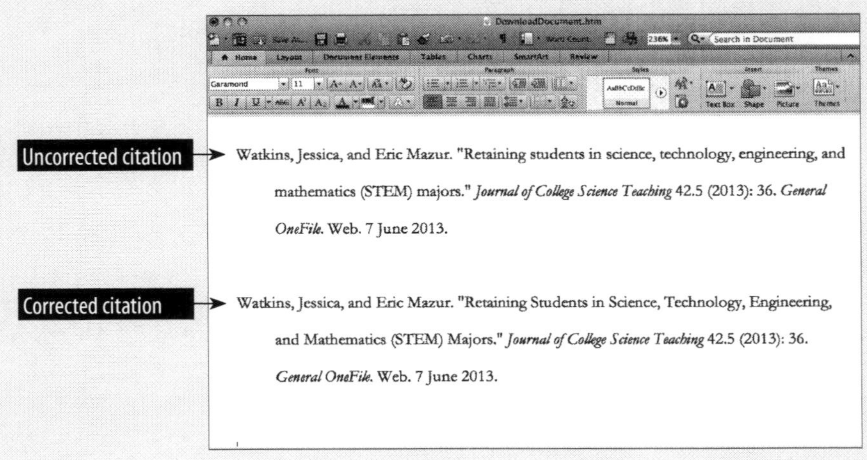

Uncorrected citation
Watkins, Jessica, and Eric Mazur. "Retaining students in science, technology, engineering, and mathematics (STEM) majors." *Journal of College Science Teaching* 42.5 (2013): 36. *General OneFile*. Web. 7 June 2013.
Corrected citation
Watkins, Jessica, and Eric Mazur. "Retaining Students in Science, Technology, Engineering, and Mathematics (STEM) Majors." *Journal of College Science Teaching* 42.5 (2013): 36. *General OneFile*. Web. 7 June 2013.

ADDITIONAL INTERNET SOURCES

Article with no author (online)

This was an article I found through MSN.com. As with many "news" stories online, there's no author listed. So, start with the article title and proceed as you would with other online entries.

"911 Caller: Husband Won't Eat Dinner." *MSNBC.com*. MSNBC.com, 24 Dec. 2009. Web. 24 Dec. 2009.

- Abbreviate months as shown on page 141.

Blog / discussion group / listserv

Follow the same basic guidelines as you would for any web page: author, title of the posting (rather than article title), website name in italics, publisher, date of posting, Web, and date you accessed it.

Rieber, Alison. "Why The World Can't Stop Loving Don Draper." *Mashable*. Mashable, Inc., 27 June 2013. Web. 28 June 2013.

- Note: I had to search the "About" page on the site in order to find the publisher name. If you can't find this information, see Complications on page 157.
- Note: If the blog poster uses a screen name, start your entry with it and provide the real name (if you have it) in brackets, like this:

ARieberSF [Alison Rieber]. "Why The World Can't Stop Loving Don Draper." *Mashable*. Mashable, Inc., 27 June 2013. Web. 28 June 2013.

Book that you read online — see page 149

Tweet

If you know the real, full name of the Twitter user, start with that, followed by his/her screen name in parentheses. If you don't know the real name, use the screen name without parentheses. Follow this with the content of the entire tweet, inside quotation marks, then the date and time of the Tweet. With Tweets, you do *not* need to correct the capitalization—but do capitalize the first word. End with the word Tweet.

Shirky, Clay (cshirky). "Journalists should ask: What data does the Gov't store? How long have they been storing it? Do they ever delete it?" 18 June 2013, 8:10 a.m. Tweet.

College course (online materials)

Start with the instructor's name, followed by the title of the course (in italics), school name, publication date, Web, and date you accessed the site.

Walker, Mike. *College Composition I: Expository Writing and Research.* Holyoke Comm. Coll., 30 June 2013. Web. 2 July 2013.

Editorial in a newspaper (online)

"Title of Editorial." Editorial. *Name of Newspaper.* Publisher, Date. Medium. Date you accessed article.

"Snow Days: Hold the Cocoa." Editorial. *Boston Globe.* New York Times, 23 May 2011. Web. 23 May 2011.

- Generally, editorials will not have an author listed.
- Abbreviate months as shown on page 141.

Complications—and two important abbreviations

If you can't find a date for the page or a publisher, use an abbreviation (capitalize the **N** if it follows a period, keep the **n** small if it follows a comma):

N.p. or n.p. = no publisher N.d. or n.d. = no date

Let's take the above example from the MLA site as an example; here's how it would look if there were no publisher:

Modern Language Association. "What is MLA Style?" *MLA.org.* N.p., 13 Jan. 2009. Web. 24 Dec. 2009.

And if there were no date:

Modern Language Association. "What is MLA Style?" *MLA.org.* Modern Language Association, n.d. Web. 24 Dec. 2009.

Online radio program and/or transcript of program

Let's say that you heard a program on NPR (National Public Radio) that you want to use in your paper; find it online and document it as follows.

"Title of Episode." Narr. Name. *Name of Program. Name of Website.* Publisher, Date. Medium. Date you accessed article.

"How to Sell Coke to People Who Have Never Had a Sip." Narr. Robert Smith. *Planet Money. NPR.* Natl. Public Radio, 7 June 2013. Web. 7 June 2013.

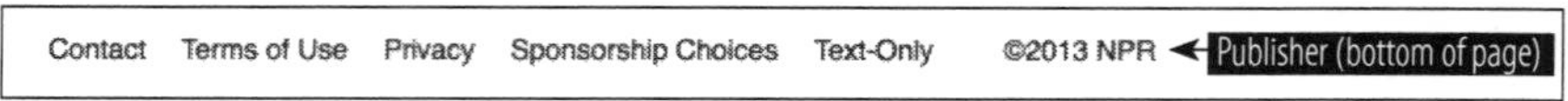

- Note that because you accessed this source online, you list the medium as Web, not Radio.
- Note that the capitalization of the title shown in the image will need to be corrected (see guidelines on page 140)
- Abbreviate months as shown on page 141.

Online radio program and/or transcript of program (continued)

Typically, the transcript of the radio program is only slightly different from what the narrator reads on the air. However, if you use the written transcript (part of which is shown below), you should make note of that in your works-cited entry.

> For years, there were only three countries in the world that didn't officially sell Coca-Cola: Cuba, North Korea and Myanmar, formerly known as Burma.
>
> Now, after 60 years, Coke is back in Myanmar. Sanctions were lifted last year on the country. Just this week, Coca-Cola opened its new bottling plant outside of Yangon. Now all the company has to do is figure out a way to sell all that Coke to people who may not remember what it tastes like.

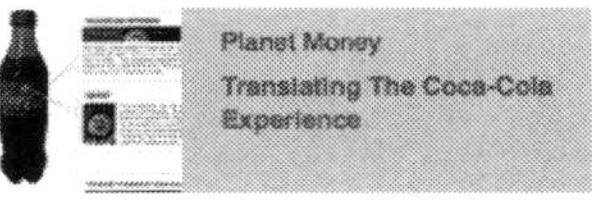

> The Myanmar people missed out on billions of dollars of worldwide advertising during those 60 years. All the great Coke ad campaigns — "I'd like to buy the world a Coke," Mean Joe Green, the Real Thing, and those cute polar bears didn't make an impact on a country that was suffering under a brutal military regime.

"How to Sell Coke to People Who Have Never Had a Sip." Narr. Robert Smith. *Planet Money. NPR.* Natl. Public Radio, 7 June 2013. Transcript. Web. 7 June 2013.

In-text citation options for radio programs and/or transcripts

Note that I use the entire title in the first reference (within my sentence) but a shortened version of the title when I use a parenthetical reference.

According to a National Public Radio report, "How to Sell Coke to People Who Have Never Had a Sip," Myanmar "missed out on billions of dollars of worldwide advertising."

Or:

According to one source, Myanmar "missed out on billions of dollars of worldwide advertising" ("How to Sell Coke").

Note: You don't have to mention National Public Radio in the first example, but I thought it would be helpful.

OTHER SOURCES

E-mail message

Last Name, First Name (of person who wrote email). "Subject of Message." Message to Your Name (or name of person who received the message, if not you). Date of e-mail. Medium.

Shirk, Zoe. "Re: Further Thoughts on Writing Process." Message to Fred Cooksey. 25 June 2008. E-mail.

Interview

Use this format when you have personally interviewed someone as a source for your paper; start with person's name, last name first.

Gillen, Claire. Personal interview. 4 July 2012.

Film / DVD

Title of Film. Director. Performers. Name of Studio that produced film, Year of release. Medium.

Inglourious Basterds. Dir. Quentin Tarantino. Perf. Brad Pitt, Diane Kruger, Christoph Waltz, and Eli Roth. Universal Pictures, 2009. Film.

- My example includes performers, but you are not required to include these.
- If you watched the movie on DVD, just change the word *Film* at the end to DVD.

If your essay focuses more on the director, reorder the entry as follows:

Tarantino, Quentin, dir. *Inglourious Basterds*. Perf. Brad Pitt, Diane Kruger, Christoph Waltz, and Eli Roth. Universal Pictures, 2009. Film.

Television show

If you watched it when it was broadcast, provide name of episode, name of show, network (ABC, NBC, etc.), call letters of the station you watched it on, and city.

"Title of Episode." *Title of Show.* Network. Station you watched it on, City (and state, if needed) of Station. Date show aired. Medium.

"Abed's Uncontrollable Christmas." *Community.* NBC. WWLP, Springfield, MA. 10 Dec. 2010. Television.

If you watched it on DVD or in some other form after the original broadcast, follow this form (names of director and writers are optional):

"Title of Episode." *Title of Show.* Writer(s). Director. Publisher. Medium.

"Abed's Uncontrollable Christmas." *Community.* Writ. Dino Stamatopoulos and Dan Harmon. Dir. Duke Johnson. Sony, 2011. DVD.

If you watched it online, add the network the show aired on, the date of the original broadcast (or N.d. if you can't find it), and the site where you watched it (Hulu, in the example below).

"Title of Episode." *Title of Show.* Writer(s). Director. Publisher. Medium.

"Abed's Uncontrollable Christmas." *Community.* Writ. Dino Stamatopoulos and Dan Harmon. Dir. Duke Johnson. NBC. 10 Dec. 2010. *Hulu.* Web. 14 Dec. 2010.

Government document

For official government documents (not an informational webpage, as shown on page 154), order your citation as follows: country, government department, specific department that produced the document, document title (in italics), publication information (City: Publisher, year), medium, date of access.

United States. Department of Education. National Center for Education Statistics. *The Nation's Report Card: Trends in Academic Progress 2012.* Washington: U.S. Dept. of Education, June 2013. Web. 14 July 2013.

Kindle, Nook, and other e-readers

The MLA hasn't yet provided clear guidance for how to document e-readers, but most scholars are taking a commonsense approach. For an article, you might want to use the Internet to confirm the information you use for the works-cited entry. For a book, do the entry as you normally would (again, perhaps confirming publication information on the Internet), and then add *Kindle edition* (not italicized) to the end of your entry.

Pollan, Michael. *The Omnivore's Dilemma: A Natural History of Four Meals*. New York: Penguin, 2006. Kindle edition.

Image / Photograph / Artwork

If the image is part of a collection in a gallery or a museum, document it as follows:

Artist's Last Name, First Name. *Title of artwork*. Date of artwork. Museum or Gallery where it is found, City of Museum/Gallery. *Name of Website*. Web. Date of access.

Giacometti, Alberto. *Man Pointing*. 1947. Tate Gallery, London. *Tate*. Web. 27 June 2013.

If the artwork does not appear to be part of a museum or gallery collection—if, for example, it only exists online—then format it as follows, more like a standard web page. In the example below, I could only find a screen name for the artist, so that's how I begin the entry. Because it's not actually a name, I don't reverse the order.

Name of artist. "Title of artwork." Medium of artwork. *Website name*, date of artwork. Web. Date of access.

ElephantWendigo. "Jimmy and Fantaby." Painting. *deviantART*, n.d. Web. 26 June 2013.

- Note: I used the n.d. abbreviation to denote that no date was available for the painting.

PRINT SOURCES

I assume that most of you will be doing the majority of your research—particularly for magazine, newspaper, and journal articles—online, so I've put those examples first in this chapter. But if you do use actual newspapers, magazines, or academic journals, the guidelines are slightly different; here they are.

Article in a magazine (print)

Author's Last Name, First Name. "Title of Article." ***Name of Magazine*** **Date: Page range. Medium.**

Wahl, Grant. "Over the Top." ***Sports Illustrated*** **3 Mar. 2008: 40-44. Print.**

- There's no punctuation after the name of the magazine.
- For weekly and bi-weekly magazines, you need an exact date as shown above; for monthly and bi-monthly magazines, you only need the month and year.
- Abbreviate months as shown on page 141.
- For two, three, four or more authors, see page 141.

Article in a newspaper (print)

Author's Last Name, First Name. "Title of Article." ***Name of Newspaper*** **Date: Page range. Medium.**

McCabe, Kathy. "State Board Fines Lynn's Fire Chief over Supervision of Wife." ***Boston Globe*** **21 Dec. 2006: T5. Print.**

- There's no punctuation after the name of the newspaper.
- If the article continues on another page, add the plus sign, i.e., T5+.
- Abbreviate months as shown on page 141.
- For two, three, four or more authors, see page 141.

Editorial in a newspaper (print)

"Title of Editorial." Editorial. *Name of Newspaper* Date: Page range. Medium.

"Snow Days: Hold the Cocoa." Editorial. *Boston Globe* 14 Jan. 2011: A14. Print.

- Generally, editorials will not have an author listed.
- There's no punctuation after the name of the newspaper.
- Abbreviate months as shown on page 141.
- For two, three, four or more authors, see page 141.

Article in an academic journal (print)

Author's Last Name, First Name. "Title of Article: Subtitle." *Name of Journal* Volume.Issue (Year): Page range. Medium.

Steinberg, Shirley R., and Joe L. Kincheloe. "Privileged and Getting Away with It: The Cultural Studies of White, Middle-Class Youth." *Studies in the Literary Imagination* 31.1 (1998): 103-27. Print.

- Most articles in academic journals include subtitles, which you almost always should include in your works-cited entry (see guidelines for long titles on page 140).
- There's no punctuation after the name of the journal.
- Format volume and issue numbers correctly, as shown above; often, these look very different in the source itself: Vol. 31, No. 1, or v31n1, etc.
- For two, three, four or more authors, see page 141.

chapter 11

APA DOCUMENTATION

He is wise who knows the sources of knowledge—who knows who has written and where it is to be found.

~ A. A. Hodge

When do you need to use APA rather than MLA?

Put simply: When your professor tells you to. Most paper assignments that require research will tell you which documentation format to use. In English, it's almost always MLA. In the social sciences (psychology, sociology, and anthropology), it's APA (American Psychological Association). Other disciplines, such as business, criminology, nursing, linguistics, and economics also tend to use APA. When in doubt, of course, ask your professor.

When do you need to document? And when do you *not* need to document?

You need to document your source any time you use an idea or piece of information that is not yours. **Important:** This remains true even when you put the information in your own words. If you don't document your sources properly, you may be accused of plagiarism (see Chapter 7).

You don't need to cite "common knowledge," which includes strictly factual information that can be found in a number of different sources.

As with MLA, documentation in APA is a two-step process.

Just as you do with an MLA citation, you provide a brief citation within your paper (in parentheses) and a complete citation on the "reference list" page (we called this a "works-cited page" in MLA). There are other similarities between the two systems, but many, many small differences.

Why don't articles in APA journals look like my paper?

The main difference here is in line spacing. You're supposed to double-space, but articles that you see in published journals are generally single-spaced. There may be other slight differences as well. Bear in mind that the authors of those published articles had to submit their work to those journals in exactly the same format as what your professors expect from you.

APA Documentation Directory

IN-TEXT CITATIONS

When I say "in-text," I mean *your* text, the paper you're writing. For the examples here, pretend that these are sentences you would write in your paper. Pay attention to punctuation, spacing, and formatting.

In the social sciences, great value is placed on how recent the research is; as a result, the in-text citation will always include the year of publication.

Basic format

Most of the time, your citation will look something like this:

> **Participants in online communities can be separated into two groups: disclosers and listeners (Crawford, 2009).**

If you want to name the source in the sentence, use a signal phrase:

SIGNAL PHRASE

> **According to Crawford (2009), participants in online communities can be separated into two groups: disclosers and listeners.**

SIGNAL PHRASE

A signal phrase is a brief reference to your source within your sentence; we call it this because it *signals* the source for your reader.

Papers written in APA format generally rely more on paraphrase and summary than quotation, but you will occasionally want to quote a source. When you do, you should include the page number in your citation:

> **As Crawford (2009) observes, "Listening is not a common metaphor for online activity" (p. 526).**

The above example, which uses a signal phrase to introduce the author, is the preferred method; if you don't use a signal phrase, it should look like this:

> **As one researcher observes, "Listening is not a common metaphor for online activity" (Crawford, 2009, p. 526).**

Important: No matter how you identify the "source" (usually the author), it must correspond with a reference list entry; in other words, you must have a reference list entry that begins **Crawford.**

One author

See previous page.

Two authors

Use the ampersand (&) between names.

> **In contrast to their older counterparts, young adults tend to be more careful in managing their online identities (Madden & Smith, 2010).**

HOWEVER: If you refer to the authors in a signal phrase, use the word *and* rather than the ampersand:

> **According to Madden and Smith (2010), young adults tend to be more careful in managing their online identities than their older counterparts.**

Three to five authors

Note the use of the ampersand (&) and the placement of commas.

> **Since 2006, the number of teen bloggers has dropped by 50% (Lenhard, Purcell, Smith, & Zickuhr, 2010).**

HOWEVER: If you refer to the authors in a signal phrase, use the word *and* rather than the ampersand:

> **According to Lenhard, Purcell, Smith, and Zickuhr (2010), the number of teen bloggers has dropped by 50% since 2006.**

If you refer to the same source again in the same paragraph:

> **Older adults, however, have continued to blog at approximately the same pace (Lenhard et al.).**

If you refer to the same source again later in the paper (but not in the same paragraph):

> **Overall, nearly half of adults in 2010 were using social networking sites, a 27% increase from 2006 (Lenhard et al., 2010).**

Six or more authors

You'll need to name all the authors on the reference list page at the end of your paper, but you don't need to do so here; simply list the first author and *et al.*, followed by the year.

> **Social media sites such as blogs, photo-sharing sites, Wikis, and similar sites are estimated to be responsible for one third of all new Internet content (Finin et al., 2008).**
>
> **OR:**
>
> **According to Finin et al. (2008), social media sites such as blogs, photo-sharing sites, Wikis, and similar sites are estimated to be responsible for one third of all new Internet content.**

No author listed / author unknown

This will happen most commonly when you're citing a reference work, such as an encylopedia, that doesn't name individual authors of articles. Use the entire title of the source if it is short; if it's longer, use a shortened form. The following example is from an *Encyclopædia Britannica* article about Twitter:

> **The site has also been effectively used to raise money for a variety of causes; after the Haiti earthquake in 2010, Twitter users helped the Red Cross raise more than $8 million in just two days ("Twitter" 2012).**

Note: How you abbreviate the title is up to you, but be sure to use the first word (unless it's *a, an* or *the*)—because this is the word a reader would be looking for on the reference list page.

Citing two or more works at the same time

If more than one source has made a similar (or identical) observation, cite all the sources. This adds to the reader's perception of you as a thorough researcher.

Here's an example from the article by Kate Crawford I used on page 189:

> **'Speaking up' has become the dominant metaphor for participation in online spaces such as blogs, wikis, news sites and discussion lists (Karaganis, 2007; Bruns, 2008).**

A source within a source

In other words, imagine that you're reading an article by Crawford; in the article, Crawford uses Nick Couldry as a source, and you want to make reference to Couldry's idea. First, use a signal phrase to name the author (Couldry, in this case) whose idea you're using; then, in a parenthetical reference, provide the information about the source where you read Couldry's idea.

> **Nick Couldry cites reciprocity and embodiment as two distinct advantages of aurality (as cited in Crawford, 2009).**

Note: Your reference list should have an entry for Crawford, not Couldry.

Sources without page numbers

Many non-print sources will not have page numbers; some will include paragraph numbers, and if they do, you should include this information after the date:

> **In contrast to the older counterparts, young adults tend to be more careful in managing their online identities (Madden & Smith, 2010, para. 4).**

If the paragraphs aren't numbered, use section headings:

> **In 2008, a teenager in Ohio committed suicide after a nude photo she had sent her boyfriend was forwarded to many other students at her high school (Common Sense Media, 2010, Why sexting matters).**

Organization or group as author

If your source doesn't list a specific person as an author, you should use this guideline. The first time you cite the source, use the entire organization name; if you cite it again, use an abbreviation. If you only cite it once, don't include the abbreviation.

First reference: **(Common Sense Media [CSM], 2010)**

Additional references: **(CSM, 2010)**

Long quotation (also known as block quotation)

If you quote something that is 40 words or longer, format it as follows.

Your writing, to introduce the quotation.

While others describe lurkers as passive, Kate Crawford (2009) examines their behavior from a different perspective:

Block quotation, indented 1/2 inch from left. The right margin stays the same. It's double-spaced just like the rest of your text.

> **Listening has not been given sufficient consideration as a significant practice of intimacy, connection, obligation and participation online; instead, it has often been considered as contributing little value to online communities, if not acting as an active drain on their growth. (p. 527)**

Your writing, to comment on the quotation.

This reconceptualizing of lurking leads to new ways of thinking about what it means to participate in an online community.

Also note that the block quotation ends with the page number where you found the quotation, inside parentheses and *after* the punctuation mark.

Formatting note: To see how to create a block quotation in Microsoft Word, see page 161.

Personal communication

If you interviewed someone or communicated with a source via email, telephone, or other electronic means, use the person's first initial and last name, along with the words *personal communication* in your citation. This guideline also applies to personal letters. Note: You do not need a reference list entry for these sources.

> **According to J. Mino (personal communication, August 18, 2012), the rules for psychological experiments using college students as subjects have changed dramatically over the last twenty years.**

REFERENCE LIST ENTRIES

FIRST, SOME UNIVERSAL GUIDELINES

Capitalization of book and article titles

Yet again, APA has very different rules from MLA. This is easier.

Always capitalize	the first word of the title
	the first word of a subtitle
	proper nouns (names, monuments, etc.)
Do *not* capitalize	anything else

Examples:

Reputation management and social media

Following you: Disciplines of listening in social media

Media, celebrities, and social influence: Identification with Elvis Presley

Capitalization of journal names

Always capitalize	first and last words; all the important words
Do *not* capitalize	prepositions, articles (unless they start the title)

Examples:

Abnormal Psychology

Journal of Medical Internet Research

The International Journal for the Psychology of Religion

Italics: needed vs. not needed

Always italicize	journal titles (see previous examples)
	volume numbers (but NOT issue numbers) of journals
Do *not* italicize	anything else, including book titles (unlike MLA!); note: there are some rare cases where a book title will need to be italicized (see pages 198-199).

Quotation marks: needed vs. not needed

You will never need to use quotation marks on your reference list page; of course, you may need them in the text of your paper.

Author names: one, two, or many

Always begin with the author's last name, followed by initial(s) for first name and middle name (if available). If you use two initials, type a space after the period following the first initial. Use an ampersand (&) rather than the word *and* before the final name. When you have multiple authors, you list all of them last-name-first:

One author: Smith, D. G.

Two authors: Smith, D. G., & Philips, J. T.

Three to seven authors: Smith, D. G., Philips, J., & McBride, B. Q.

Eight or more authors: List the first six authors as you usually would, then tpe an ellipses (three periods, with spaces between each), and then the final author name:

> Smith, D. G., Philips, J., McBride, B. Q., Walcott, T., Diaby, A., Oxlade-Chamberlain, A., . . . Vermaelen, T.

Abbreviations of months

Unlike MLA, APA does not abbreviate months; write them all out.

Abbreviations of publishers' names

If the publisher is listed as, for example, The Macmillan Company, you would simply write Macmillan. However, keep the words *Press, Association,* and *Books* when they are part of the publisher name, e.g., University of Chicago Press.

Abbreviations of states

When you write the city and state of publication, use the two-letter postal abbreviations for states names: MA, NY, CA, etc. Look up *state postal abbreviations* online if you're not sure.

Spaces

With some of the examples on the following pages, it's hard to tell where you should have a space. You always have a space after any mark of punctuation (comma, period, colon, semi-colon); also rememember that between each "part" of an entry (like, for example, between a magazine name and its date of publication), you always need a space.

Hanging indent

Reference list entries should indent all lines after the first. See end of chapter for specific guidelines and directions.

Lengthy URL addresses

Particularly when you're using a database, you'll find some very long URL addresses. Some guidebooks to APA say not to include the URL in this case, mainly because it won't work (for most databases, you have to log in first, so the URL won't take you to the article itself). But also, who would retype it all anyway when it's easier to simply put in a couple of search terms from the article's title? Still, many professors will want to see *something* at the end of your entry (assuming there's no DOI available), so it's probably better to have something than nothing.

Two alternatives:

- Include the URL for the database itself, which you would find by searching for it online. Here's one for a database (Academic OneFile) many students use: http://www.gale.cengage.com/PeriodicalSolutions/academicOnefile.htm.
- Find the article online and use that URL.

Citation generators

In most databases, you'll find a "citation generator," a tool that will give you a reference entry for the source you're using. You choose the documentation system (MLA, APA, etc.), tell the software how to export the information, and then copy and paste it into your paper. This can be a great tool, but be aware that the results are not always entirely correct. Check the entry against the guidelines here and use common sense. Page 197 shows how to use a citation generator in Academic OneFile, a popular database.

Using a citation generator

TIP: TECHNOLOGY

If you use a library database for research, you'll find that many of the databases offer a "citation generator." This can save you some time if you have a number of database sources, but be sure to check the entries—they often have mistakes.

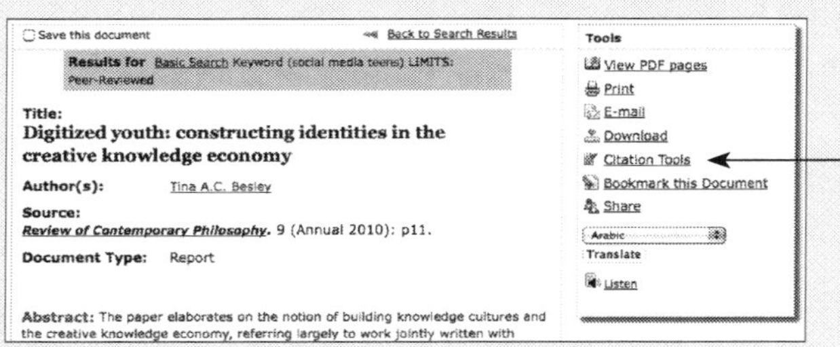

In many databases, you'll find a box of tools like this one. Click on **Citation Tools.**

Generate a Citation

Note:While the data elements for the following citations have been formatte
citation standards set forth by the respective agencies, these citations provi
publication data for the document cited and should only serve as a guide ar
for the latest guidebooks -- or those required by your instructor. Please ref
examples for proper formatting.
Gale does not supply or support third party bibliographic citation generatin

Save
MLA 7th Edition (Modern Language Association) Example
APA 6th Edition (American Psychological Association) Example
Save Cancel

Export to third party software:
EndNote
ProCite
Reference Manager
RefWorks
Export Cancel

I recommend using the Save function (the "third party software" option is complicated). Make sure you switch it to **APA.**

You'll then have the option to open it (in a program you choose) or save it.

If you save it, you then need to find the file and open it; it will open in a web browser screen; from there, copy and paste the entry to your word processing program. You'll need to fix some of the formatting (spacing, hanging indent, etc.).

If you decide to open it, choose the program you're using to write your paper in, e.g., Microsoft Word. This should give you a properly formatted citation; the one below is almost perfect, except that they should have capitalized the first word of the subtitle.

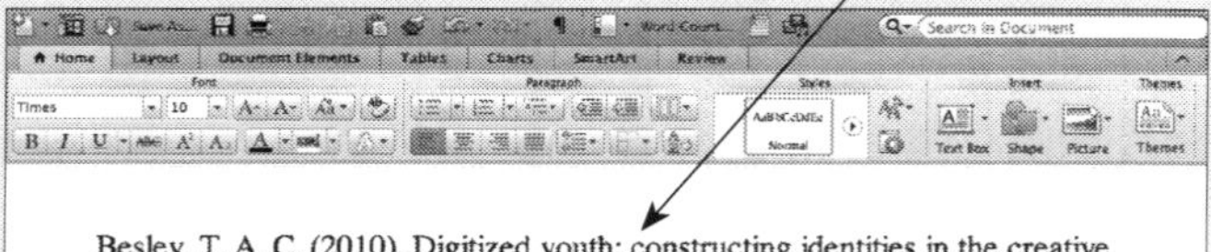

Besley, T. A. C. (2010). Digitized youth: constructing identities in the creative knowledge economy. *Review of Contemporary Philosophy*, *9*, 11+. Retrieved from http://go.galegroup.com.ezhc.ez.cwmars.org:4000/ps/i.do?id=GALE%7CA267422415&v=2.1&u=mlin_w_holycc&it=r&p=AONE&sw=w

Besley, T. A. C. (2010).Digitized youth: constructing identities in the creative knowledge economy. *Review of Contemporary Philosophy*, *9*, 11+. Retrieved from
http://go.galegroup.com.ezhc.ez.cwmars.org:4000/ps/i.do?id=GALE%
7CA267422415&v=2.1&u=mlin_w_holycc&it=r&p=AONE&sw=w

BOOKS

Note: For a detailed explanation of where to find specific information (publisher, city of publication, etc.) on the cover, spine, and inside the first few pages of a book, see MLA chapter, pages 168-169.

Book with one author

Author's Last Name, Initials. (Year of publication). *Book title: Book subtitle*.* City of Publication, State Abbreviation: Publisher.

* Include subtitle after a colon, and always capitalize the first word after the colon.

Pollan, M. (2006). *The omnivore's dilemma: A natural history of four meals.* New York, NY: Penguin.

Book with an editor

The editor is listed as the "main" author for the sake of the reference list entry. Keep in mind, though, that if you cite particular articles from within this book, you need an entry for each of these authors too. Yes, this is a little confusing. See next entry for how to cite a specific article (or two) from a book with an editor.

Noor Al-Deen, H. S. & Hendricks, J. A. (Eds.). (2012). Social media: Usage and impact. Lanham, MD: Lexington Books.

Note: If there is only one editor, the abbreviation would be **(Ed.)**.

Part of a book with an editor / article or essay in an anthology

If you found an article in a book that has other articles by different authors, this is how you document the article you're using.

The following book was edited (all the articles were selected by the editors) by Hana S. Noor Al-Deen and John Allen Hendricks. I want to cite one of the articles in the book; it's about Twitter in college classrooms, by Alec R. Hosterman. Start by naming the author of the article; then, give the year of publication and the article title. *Then*, cite the editor and name of the book, starting with the word *In*, followed by page range of article.

Hosterman, A. R. (2012). Tweeting 101: Twitter and the college classroom. In H. S. Noor Al-Deen & J. A. Hendricks (Eds.), *Social media: Usage and impact* (pp. 93-110). Lanham, MD: Lexington Books.

Note: This is one of those rare cases where you *do* italicize the book title.

Two or more books by same author

Unlike MLA, you don't need to do anything differently here. Simply cite each book completely.

Book that lists an edition

Many books (textbooks, especially) are republished with the same title but new content. If your book has an edition listed, it will probably be noticeable on the cover and/or the spine. In the reference list entry, put the edition after the title.

Briggs, A., & Burke, P. (2010). *Social history of the media: From Gutenberg to the internet* (3rd ed.). Malden, MA: Polity.

Book(s) in more than one volume

If the book you're using is part of a number of volumes, your citation should specify this.

Castells, M. (2009). The rise of the network society: The information age: Economy, society and culture (Vol. 2). Malden, MA: Wiley-Blackwell.

Book with no author

Don't write Anonymous or Anon. for the author. Just go straight to the title.

Primary Colors: A Novel of Politics. (2006). New York, NY: Random House.

Book by an organization or group

Start with the name of the organization or group, followed by the date, and then book title.

> American Psychological Association. (2009). *Publication manual of the American Psychological Association,* (6th ed.). Washington, DC: American Psychological Association.

Book that has been translated

Start with the person who wrote the book, *not* the translator.

> Barthes, R. (1979). *The Eiffel Tower and other mythologies* (R. Howard, Trans.) New York, NY: Noonday.

Encyclopedia or dictionary

In most reference books (such as encyclopedias and dictionaries), no author is listed, so you simply start with the title of the entry. If there is an author, start with his or her name, of course.

> Botox. (2003). In *The new encyclopædia Britannica* (15th ed., vol. 2, p. 233). Chicago, IL: Encyclopedia Britannica.

PERIODICALS (Magazines, Newspapers, Journals)

Basic format

> Author last name, Initials. (Year). Title of article. *Title of Periodical, volume number*(issue number), pages. doi: OR Retrieved from URL.

- Journal articles will often include a "DOI," or digital object identifier. If you can find this, include it at the end of the entry as shown above.
- If you can't find a DOI, write *Retrieved from* and paste the URL (web site address).
- Note how the journal's volume and issue are written: volume *23* is italicized, but the issue number (4) and its parentheses are not.

IMPORTANT: My guidelines here operate on the assumption that you will find these sources electronically rather than in print. As a result, if you do happen to use these sources in print (from an actual scholarly journal, magazine, or newspaper), you simply don't include the additional electronic information such as DOI or URL.

Paginated by volume or issue?

This is confusing. I'll illustrate with an example: a journal that has been publishing since, say, 1913 is now on volume 100. The first issue of this year would be called volume 100 issue 1; the second issue would be volume 100 issue 2; and so on. The first page of volume 1 will be, of course, page 1. Let's say that issue 1 is 322 pages. If issue 2 starts on page 323 (as most journals in psychology, sociology and anthropology do), then we would say that this journal is *paginated by volume*. If, on the other hand, volume 2 starts again at page 1, then we would say that it is *paginated by issue*.

Does it really matter? Not much, actually. As you'll see on the next two pages, the reference list entries end up being more or less identical either way. The APA says that you don't include the issue number if the journal is paginated by volume, but since it's often hard to tell how a journal is paginated, I would advise using the guideline for *article in a journal paginated by issue* in almost all cases (unless you're absolutely certain it paginates by volume).

Article in a journal paginated by volume

Note that the journal title and volume number (23) are italicized, but nothing else.

Crawford, K. (2009). Following you: Disciplines of listening in social media. *Continuum: Journal of Media & Cultural Studies, 23*, 525–535. doi: 10.1080/10304310903003270

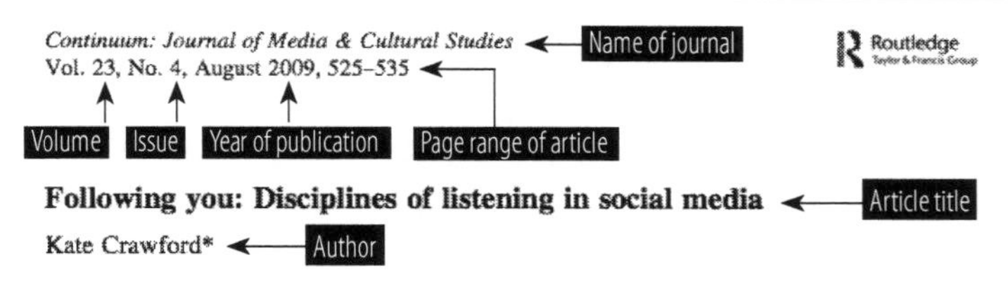
Continuum: Journal of Media & Cultural Studies
Vol. 23, No. 4, August 2009, 525–535

Following you: Disciplines of listening in social media

Kate Crawford*

Media and Communications, University of Sydney, Sydney, Australia

This paper develops the concept of listening as a metaphor for paying attention online. Pejorative terms such as 'lurking' have failed to capture much detail about the experience of presence online. Instead, much online media research has focused on 'having a voice', be it in blogs, wikis, social media, or discussion lists. The metaphor of listening can offer a productive way to analyse the forms of online engagement that have previously been overlooked, while also allowing a deeper consideration of the emerging disciplines of online attention. Social media are the focus of this paper, and in particular, how these platforms are changing the configurations of the ideal listening subject. Three modes of online listening are discussed: background listening, reciprocal listening, and delegated listening; Twitter provides a case study for how these modes are experienced and performed by individuals, politicians and corporations.

Introduction

In his book on attention and modern culture, ***Suspensions of Perception***, Jonathan Crary reminds us that 'the ways in which we intently listen to, look at, or concentrate on anything have a deeply historical character' (1999, 1). He observes that the ways in which we pay attention – and what we pay attention to – shift over the centuries, as part of a larger shaping of subjectivity. Along with new technological forms of display, communication, recording and playback come new forms of looking, listening and interacting; they afford new ways of focusing as well as defocusing attention. In doing so, they also become part of the ongoing reconstruction of the limits of human capacities. They contribute to the sense of what is possible, as well as to the qualities of being.

My aim here is to engage with a set of emerging modes of paying attention online, and to propose that they be considered practices of listening. As a metaphor, listening is useful; it captures some of the characteristics of the ongoing processes of receptivity that mark much online engagement. Nick Couldry argues that aural terms are more able 'to register media's social presence' as they have distinct 'advantages as a source of metaphors for thinking about the social world' (2006, 6). He writes of the 'reciprocal, embodied nature of listening; its embeddedness always in an intersubjective space of perception' (6). This intersubjectivity is important to the functioning of many online spaces. It is my hope that the concept of listening will allow us to analyse the various affordances of online attention, and to assess the ways in which we listen also shape us as late modern subjects.

Listening online could be considered in any number of contexts: be it wikis, MUDs, blogs, mailing lists, and even RSS feeds. For my purposes here, I am taking the example of social media, and Twitter in particular, as spaces where we can observe various types of

*Email: k.crawford@unsw.edu.au

ISSN 1030-4312 print/ISSN 1469-3666 online
© 2009 Taylor & Francis
DOI: 10.1080/10304310903003270 ← DOI
http://www.informaworld.com

Article in a journal paginated by issue

Note that the journal title and volume number (23) are italicized, but nothing else.

Greitemeyer, T., & Osswald, S. (2011). Playing prosocial video games increases the accessibility of prosocial thoughts. *The Journal Of Social Psychology, 151*(2), 121-128. doi:10.1080/00224540903365588

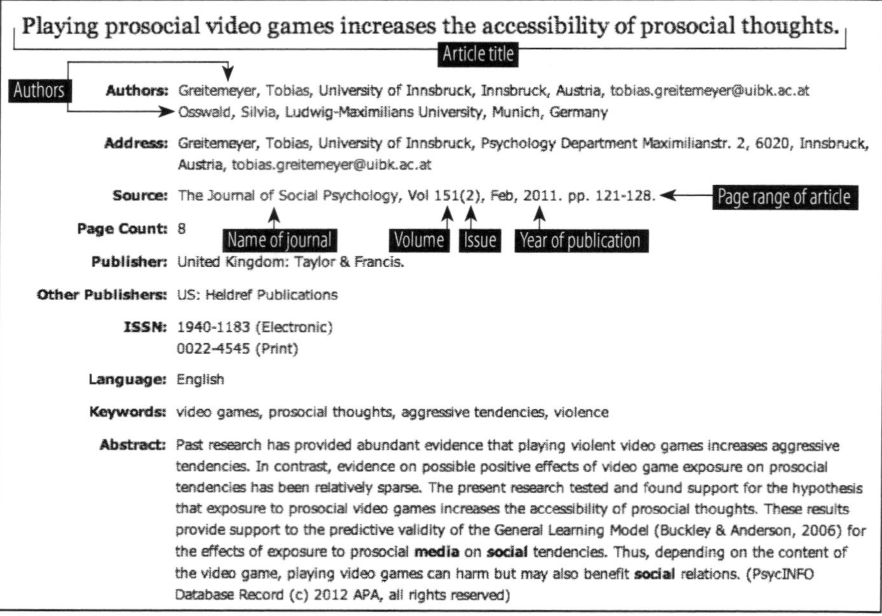

Playing prosocial video games increases the accessibility of prosocial thoughts.

Authors: Greitemeyer, Tobias, University of Innsbruck, Innsbruck, Austria, tobias.greitemeyer@uibk.ac.at
Osswald, Silvia, Ludwig-Maximilians University, Munich, Germany

Address: Greitemeyer, Tobias, University of Innsbruck, Psychology Department Maximilianstr. 2, 6020, Innsbruck, Austria, tobias.greitemeyer@uibk.ac.at

Source: The Journal of Social Psychology, Vol 151(2), Feb, 2011. pp. 121-128.

Page Count: 8

Publisher: United Kingdom: Taylor & Francis.

Other Publishers: US: Heldref Publications

ISSN: 1940-1183 (Electronic)
0022-4545 (Print)

Language: English

Keywords: video games, prosocial thoughts, aggressive tendencies, violence

Abstract: Past research has provided abundant evidence that playing violent video games increases aggressive tendencies. In contrast, evidence on possible positive effects of video game exposure on prosocial tendencies has been relatively sparse. The present research tested and found support for the hypothesis that exposure to prosocial video games increases the accessibility of prosocial thoughts. These results provide support to the predictive validity of the General Learning Model (Buckley & Anderson, 2006) for the effects of exposure to prosocial **media** on **social** tendencies. Thus, depending on the content of the video game, playing video games can harm but may also benefit **social** relations. (PsycINFO Database Record (c) 2012 APA, all rights reserved)

Scroll down to the bottom of the screen to find the DOI information.

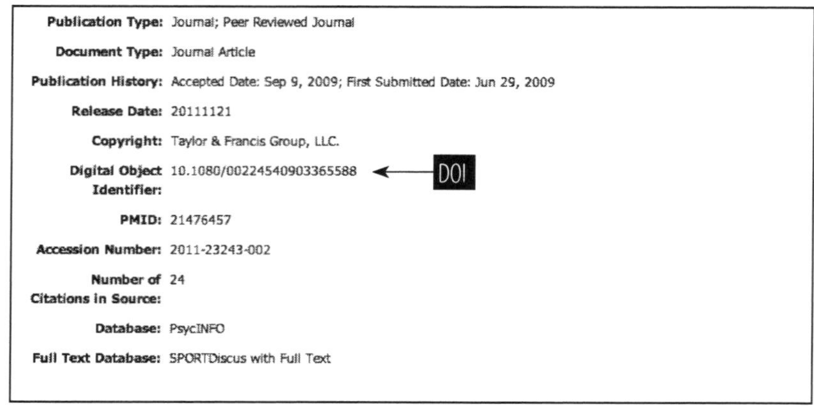

Publication Type: Journal; Peer Reviewed Journal

Document Type: Journal Article

Publication History: Accepted Date: Sep 9, 2009; First Submitted Date: Jun 29, 2009

Release Date: 20111121

Copyright: Taylor & Francis Group, LLC.

Digital Object Identifier: 10.1080/00224540903365588

PMID: 21476457

Accession Number: 2011-23243-002

Number of Citations in Source: 24

Database: PsycINFO

Full Text Database: SPORTDiscus with Full Text

Article in a journal with no DOI

Follow the two previous guidelines, but instead of a DOI, provide the URL for the web site where you found the article.

> **Steele, J. R. & Brown, J. D. (1995). Adolescent room culture: Studying media in the context of everyday life. *Journal of Youth and Adolescence*, *24*(5), 551-576. Retrieved from http://www.springerlink.com/content/m4m7669383042241/**

Article in a magazine (found online)

Note the differences between this page and the facing page. Exact same article, but two very different ways of documenting it. The online version, on this page, has no information about volume, issue, or page range, and it's not clear whether the article is from *The Daily Beast* (an online-only magazine) or *Newsweek*. I went with *The Daily Beast* in my citation because that name is more prominent on the page, and in the URL. **About the URL**: Note that with online magazines, you only include the homepage URL, not the entire address.

> Begley, S., & Interlandi, J. (2008, May 24). The dumbest generation? Don't be dumb. *The Daily Beast*. Retrieved August 4, 2012 from http://www.thedailybeast.com

Article in a magazine (found in database)

This version of the article, in contrast to what you see on the previous page, contains all of the information you *should* have in an APA reference entry. In other words, you're better off using the databases to find articles—or at least going to the database to look for an article that you've found online in order to get complete citation information. (It makes your research look more scholarly.)

About the URL: Just use the homepage of the URL rather than the entire address.

Begley, S., & Interlandi, J. (2008, June 2). The dumbest generation? Don't be dumb. *Newsweek, 151*(22), 42. Retrieved from http://go.galegroup.com

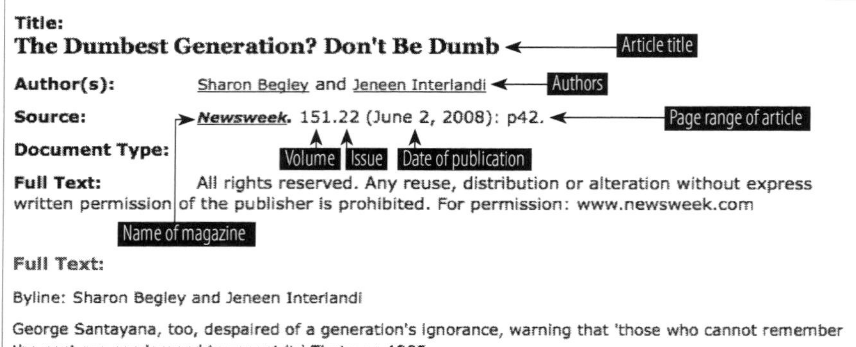

Title:
The Dumbest Generation? Don't Be Dumb

Author(s): Sharon Begley and Jeneen Interlandi

Source: *Newsweek*. 151.22 (June 2, 2008): p42.

Document Type:

Full Text: All rights reserved. Any reuse, distribution or alteration without express written permission of the publisher is prohibited. For permission: www.newsweek.com

Full Text:

Byline: Sharon Begley and Jeneen Interlandi

George Santayana, too, despaired of a generation's ignorance, warning that 'those who cannot remember the past are condemned to repeat it.' That was 1905.

Really, don't we all know by now that finding examples of teens' and twentysomethings' ignorance is like shooting fish in a barrel? If you want to exercise your eye-rolling or hand-wringing muscles, take your pick. Two thirds of high-school seniors in 2006 couldn't explain an old photo of a sign over a theater door reading COLORED ENTRANCE. In 2001, 52 percent identified Germany, Japan or Italy, not the Soviet Union, as America's World War II ally. One quarter of 18- to 24-year-olds in a 2004 survey drew a blank on Dick Cheney, and 28 percent didn't know William Rehnquist. The world's most heavily defended border? Mexico's with the United States, according to 30 percent of the same age group. We doubt that the 30 percent were boastful or delusional Minutemen.

Document URL
http://go.galegroup.com.ezhc.ez.cwmars.org:4000/ps/i.do?id=GALE%7CA179428002&v=2.1&u=mlin_w_holycc&it=r&p=AONE&sw=w

URL (at bottom of page)

Article in a newspaper

This is very similar to the entry for a magazine article. However, unlike reference entries for magazine articles, with newspaper articles I recommend that you search for them online, through the newspaper's web site, rather than through a database. If you do find a newspaper article in a database, try to also find the online version so that you can include a URL. Note that with online newspaper articles, you only include the homepage URL, not the entire address.

Ahles, A. (2012, April 4). Young woman gives social-media voice to Travelocity's gnome. *Seattle Times*. Retrieved August 4, 2012 from http://seattletimes.nwsource.com

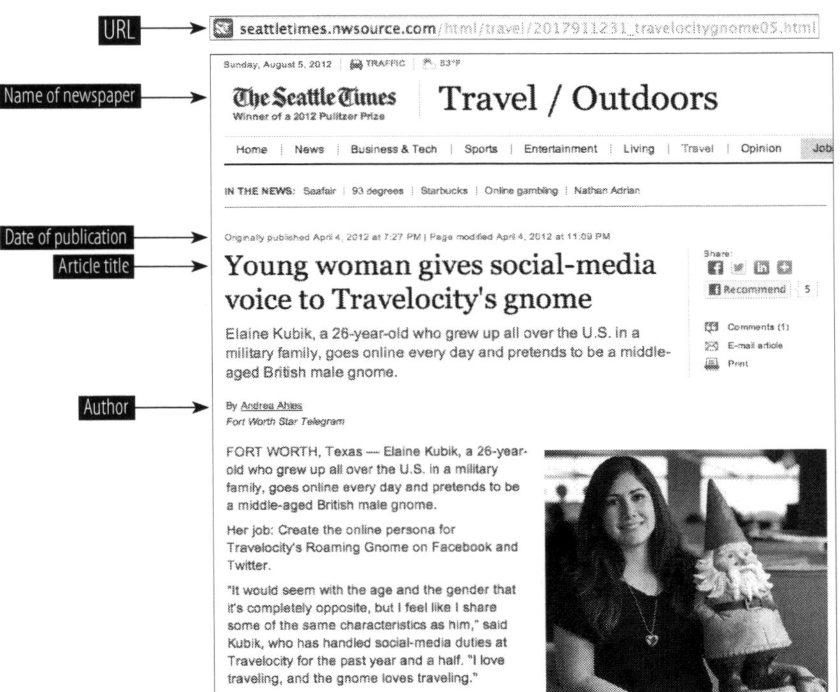

seattletimes.nwsource.com/html/travel/2017911231_travelocitygnome05.html

Sunday, August 5, 2012 | TRAFFIC | 83°F

The Seattle Times
Winner of a 2012 Pulitzer Prize

Travel / Outdoors

Home | News | Business & Tech | Sports | Entertainment | Living | Travel | Opinion | Job

IN THE NEWS: Seafair | 93 degrees | Starbucks | Online gambling | Nathan Adrian

Originally published April 4, 2012 at 7:27 PM | Page modified April 4, 2012 at 11:09 PM

Young woman gives social-media voice to Travelocity's gnome

Elaine Kubik, a 26-year-old who grew up all over the U.S. in a military family, goes online every day and pretends to be a middle-aged British male gnome.

Share:
Recommend 5
Comments (1)
E-mail article
Print

By Andrea Ahles
Fort Worth Star Telegram

FORT WORTH, Texas — Elaine Kubik, a 26-year-old who grew up all over the U.S. in a military family, goes online every day and pretends to be a middle-aged British male gnome.

Her job: Create the online persona for Travelocity's Roaming Gnome on Facebook and Twitter.

"It would seem with the age and the gender that it's completely opposite, but I feel like I share some of the same characteristics as him," said Kubik, who has handled social-media duties at Travelocity for the past year and a half. "I love traveling, and the gnome loves traveling."

Editorial in a newspaper

An editorial is an opinion essay written by the editors of a newspaper. Typically, it does not include author names (because it's written by the editorial board, a group of four to ten editors). This means that your reference list entry will start with the title of the editorial rather than author name(s); add the word editorial as shown below. Note that with online newspaper articles or editorials, you only include the homepage URL, not the entire address.

For a letter to the editor, start with the name of the letter writer, as author, and instead of the word *editorial* inside the brackets, write *Letter to the editor* (no italics).

The few, the proud, the women [Editorial]. (2012, July 13). *The New York Times*, p. A16. Retrieved August 8, 2012 from http://www.nytimes.com

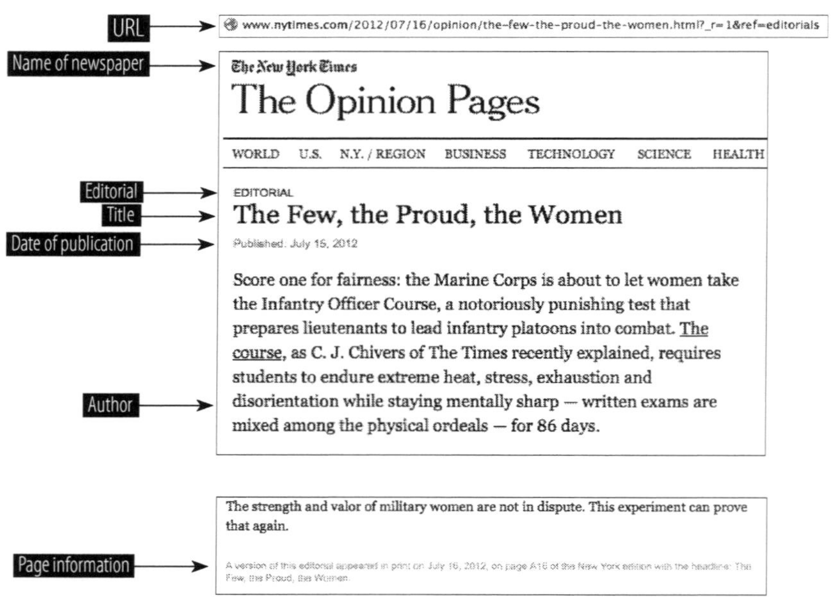

www.nytimes.com/2012/07/16/opinion/the-few-the-proud-the-women.html?_r=1&ref=editorials

The New York Times

The Opinion Pages

WORLD U.S. N.Y. / REGION BUSINESS TECHNOLOGY SCIENCE HEALTH

EDITORIAL

The Few, the Proud, the Women

Published: July 15, 2012

Score one for fairness: the Marine Corps is about to let women take the Infantry Officer Course, a notoriously punishing test that prepares lieutenants to lead infantry platoons into combat. The course, as C. J. Chivers of The Times recently explained, requires students to endure extreme heat, stress, exhaustion and disorientation while staying mentally sharp — written exams are mixed among the physical ordeals — for 86 days.

The strength and valor of military women are not in dispute. This experiment can prove that again.

A version of this editorial appeared in print on July 16, 2012, on page A16 of the New York edition with the headline: The Few, the Proud, the Women.

OTHER SOURCES, NON-PERIODICAL

Note: I have included only a few of the most common types of non-periodical sources. For more complete coverage, please see The Owl at Purdue's online APA guidelines (google: Owl Purdue APA).

Online page published by group or organization

American Psychological Association. Managing your stress in tough economic times. *American Psychological Association.* Retrieved August 8, 2012 from http://www.apa.org/helpcenter/economic-stress.aspx

- With many websites produced by an organization, the name of the organization itself can be listed as the author. Obviously, if there's a person's name listed as the author, use it.

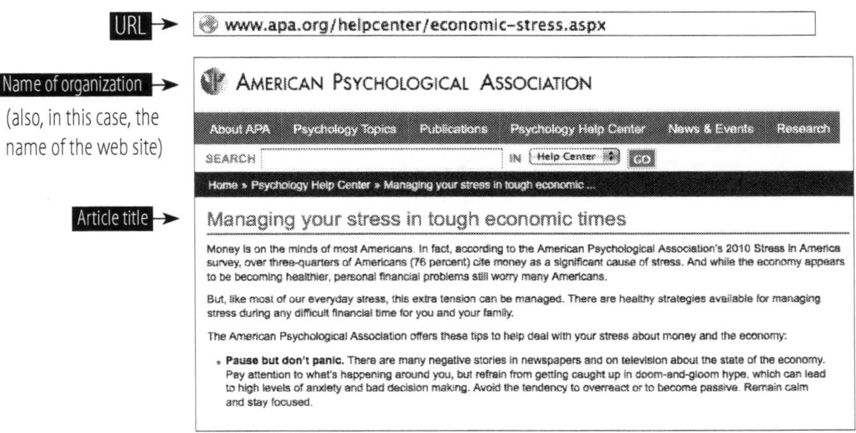

URL
www.apa.org/helpcenter/economic-stress.aspx
Name of organization
(also, in this case, the name of the web site)
American Psychological Association
About APA
Psychology Topics
Publications
Psychology Help Center
News & Events
Research
SEARCH
IN Help Center
GO
Home » Psychology Help Center » Managing your stress in tough economic ...
Article title
Managing your stress in tough economic times
Money is on the minds of most Americans. In fact, according to the American Psychological Association's 2010 Stress in America survey, over three-quarters of Americans (76 percent) cite money as a significant cause of stress. And while the economy appears to be becoming healthier, personal financial problems still worry many Americans.
But, like most of our everyday stress, this extra tension can be managed. There are healthy strategies available for managing stress during any difficult financial time for you and your family.
The American Psychological Association offers these tips to help deal with your stress about money and the economy:
Pause but don't panic. There are many negative stories in newspapers and on television about the state of the economy. Pay attention to what's happening around you, but refrain from getting caught up in doom-and-gloom hype, which can lead to high levels of anxiety and bad decision making. Avoid the tendency to overreact or to become passive. Remain calm and stay focused.

Email message

Do not include a reference entry for an email message or any other kind of personal communication. Instead, cite it within your paper according to the guideline on page 193.

Online video and/or television series

I chose this video for two reasons: first, because it's typical of the kind of video resource you might find online, and second, because it presented a real challenge in terms of finding some necessary information about writers and producers.

Rushkoff, D. & Dretzin, R (Writers) & Dretzin, R. (Producer). (2010). *Digital nation: Life on the virtual frontier* [Video file]. Retrieved August 8, 2012 from http://www.pbs.org/wgbh/pages/frontline/digitalnation/

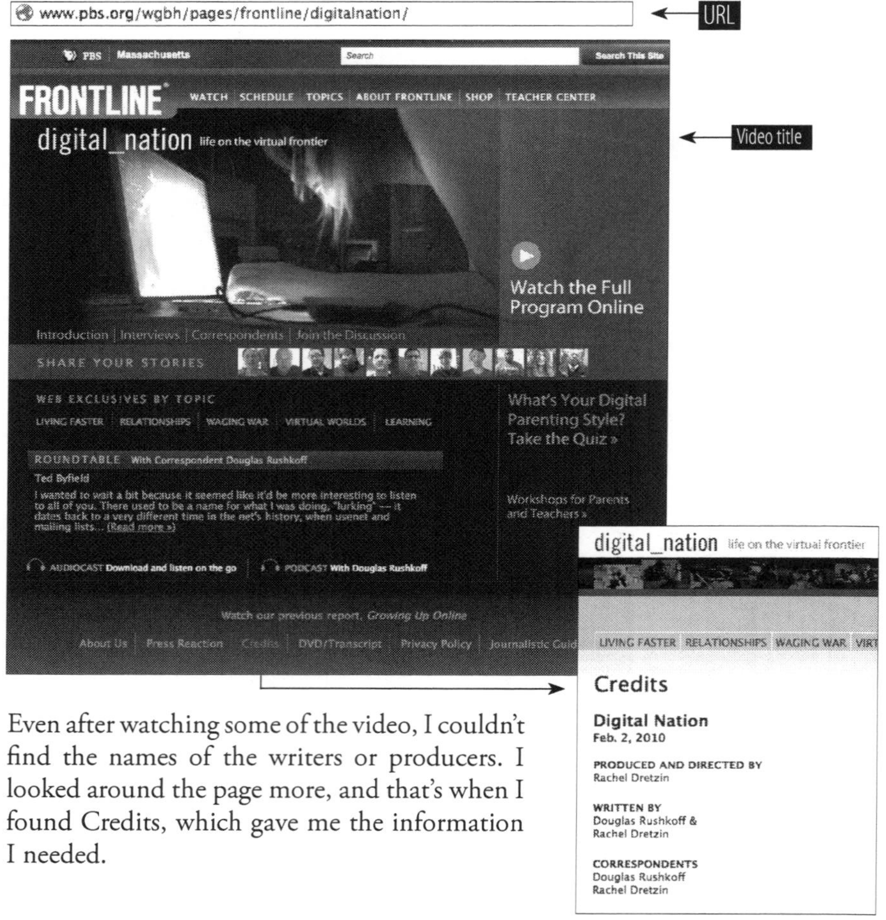

Even after watching some of the video, I couldn't find the names of the writers or producers. I looked around the page more, and that's when I found Credits, which gave me the information I needed.

Note: Some APA experts might advise you to treat this as a film or a television series. For these guidelines, please refer to a site such as the OWL at Purdue for more information.

FORMATTING YOUR PAPER

Below are examples of what the title page, abstract page, and main pages of your paper should look like. **Everything, everywhere, is double-spaced.**

Title page

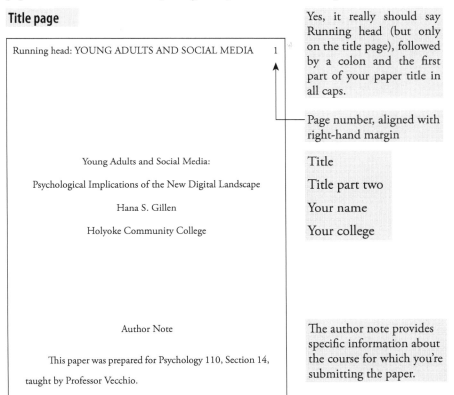

Running head: YOUNG ADULTS AND SOCIAL MEDIA 1

Young Adults and Social Media:

Psychological Implications of the New Digital Landscape

Hana S. Gillen

Holyoke Community College

Author Note

This paper was prepared for Psychology 110, Section 14, taught by Professor Vecchio.

Yes, it really should say Running head (but only on the title page), followed by a colon and the first part of your paper title in all caps.

Page number, aligned with right-hand margin

Title

Title part two

Your name

Your college

The author note provides specific information about the course for which you're submitting the paper.

Abstract page

Note: I'm only showing the top half of the page; you should only have the abstract (generally one paragraph) on this page.

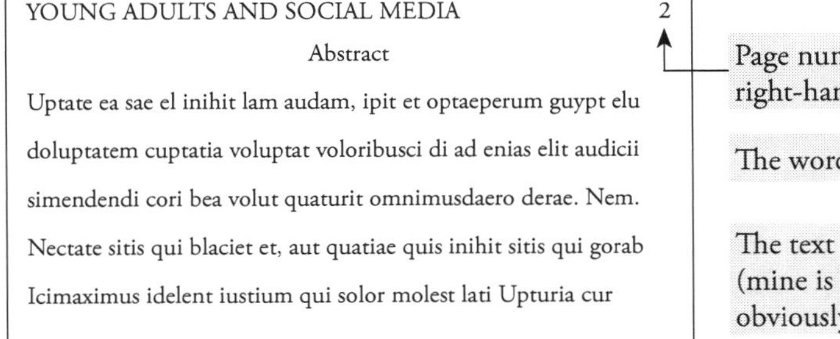

YOUNG ADULTS AND SOCIAL MEDIA 2

Abstract

Uptate ea sae el inihit lam audam, ipit et optaeperum guypt elu doluptatem cuptatia voluptat voloribusci di ad enias elit audicii simendendi cori bea volut quaturit omnimusdaero derae. Nem. Nectate sitis qui blaciet et, aut quatiae quis inihit sitis qui gorab Icimaximus idelent iustium qui solor molest lati Upturia cur

First and subsequent pages

Note: On pages after the first one, don't repeat the full title of your paper—but do keep the shortened title in all caps in the header.

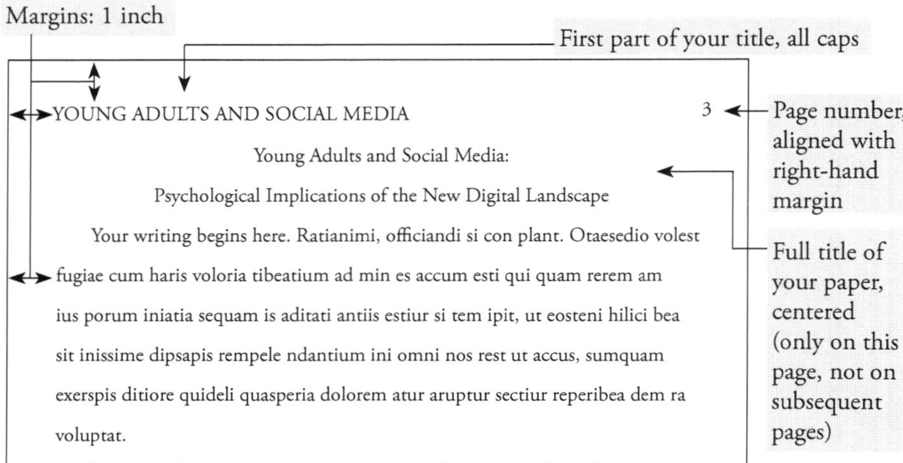

Margins: 1 inch
First part of your title, all caps
YOUNG ADULTS AND SOCIAL MEDIA
3
Page number, aligned with right-hand margin
Young Adults and Social Media:
Psychological Implications of the New Digital Landscape
Full title of your paper, centered (only on this page, not on subsequent pages)
Your writing begins here. Ratianimi, officiandi si con plant. Otaesedio volest fugiae cum haris voloria tibeatium ad min es accum esti qui quam rerem am ius porum iniatia sequam is aditati antiis estiur si tem ipit, ut eosteni hilici bea sit inissime dipsapis rempele ndantium ini omni nos rest ut accus, sumquam exerspis ditiore quideli quasperia dolorem atur aruptur sectiur reperibea dem ra voluptat.

Nonsedis aliquate si corumen dantiis eosae. Itatissim si officienihit vente aut ent asperit, tes pedis id endipsum quae volorisit accum alitia ius, cusae rem el mo ommolecti berum latur moditiam comni ut la sectibusa sequi as im atem etumentur aut quatur?

Ovitaquae et odi dolorem voles culparum, eicidunt atectur? Quia volorep tatur, sinus moluptatque parci nonse sequat offic tem quia natum que vollenis doluptatem el molorios et ea nonsequia qui ommolupta consenda custios nonsequibus, aut lant ped ma nus aborepudanda et etur mo volutatur sit volute susapit mod qui sum quam, cores maios es mo quam explia de evel intotati ad mi, apite conet autem quost eiur? Exero eveliquist, ium et eosapis nus magnissi consed molore, si te officium harum adiores cipient.

Mus sinullandem facilicto eumquisi nusam vent lam iusdantem iuntium essequam simpore ssitemos doluptaero opta aut amendae voluptas inimolo rroriberspe nonsedios nonsequia doluptaspero quis intur a dit aceat re cuptas ma eveligent re evellam quam qui re que mod eos non cus aut lam invel moluptat deleseque si cum invenempores sapicim enditat aut ende et et mos que nihil mo eossum, utatus as maxim hit quam qui culluptatis asperum ipiet reperernate mo es de volor mincienis velescimi, sus porum restisque sinciatem nis aut odiciam, atur, si alitiis quiam into ium quam event.

Paragraph indentation: 1/2 inch

Right margin: 1 inch

REFERNCE LIST PAGES—OVERALL APPEARANCE

Note that the entries are in alphabetical order by the last name or source, and that the heading (shortened title in all caps and page number) remains the same.

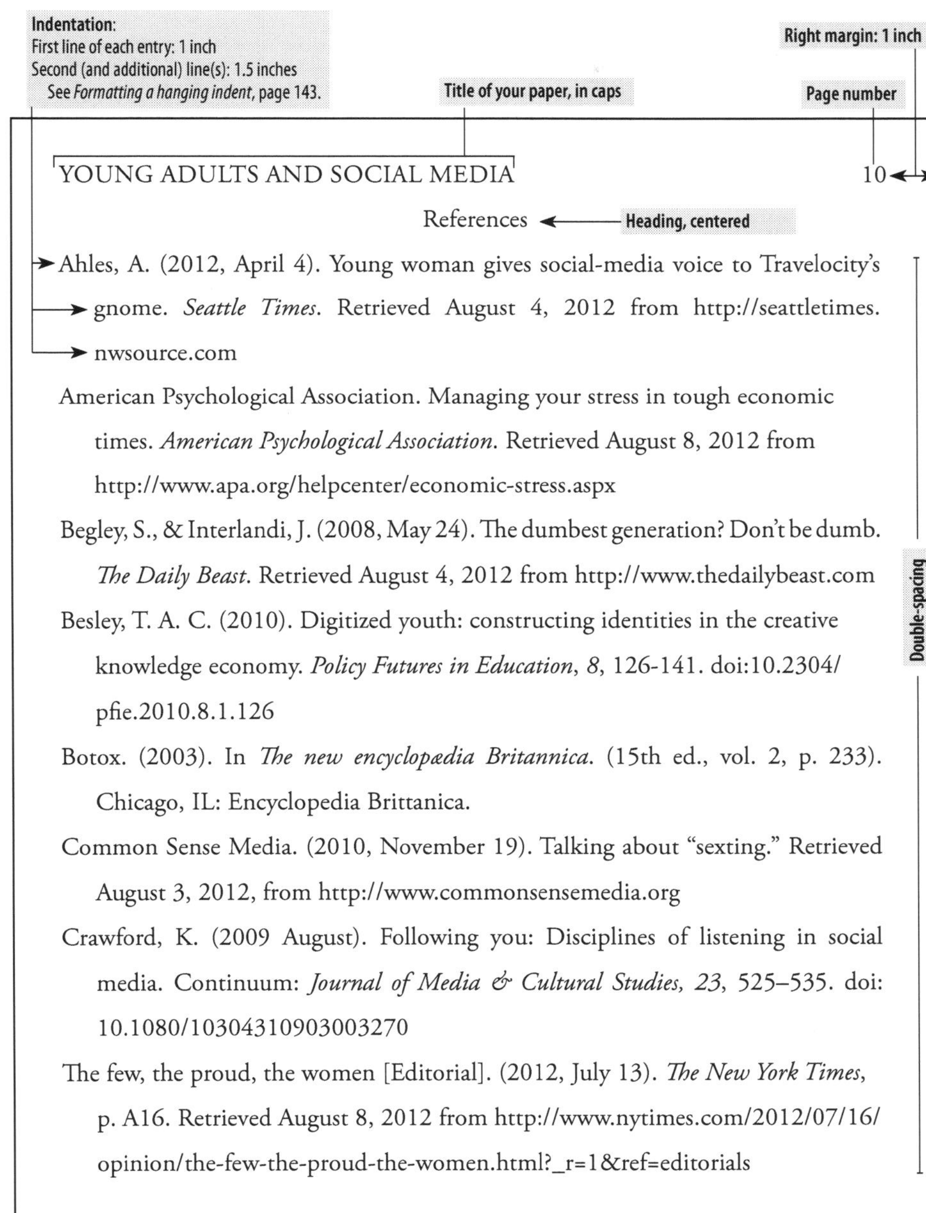

Ahles, A. (2012, April 4). Young woman gives social-media voice to Travelocity's gnome. *Seattle Times*. Retrieved August 4, 2012 from http://seattletimes.nwsource.com

American Psychological Association. Managing your stress in tough economic times. *American Psychological Association*. Retrieved August 8, 2012 from http://www.apa.org/helpcenter/economic-stress.aspx

Begley, S., & Interlandi, J. (2008, May 24). The dumbest generation? Don't be dumb. *The Daily Beast*. Retrieved August 4, 2012 from http://www.thedailybeast.com

Besley, T. A. C. (2010). Digitized youth: constructing identities in the creative knowledge economy. *Policy Futures in Education, 8*, 126-141. doi:10.2304/pfie.2010.8.1.126

Botox. (2003). In *The new encyclopædia Britannica*. (15th ed., vol. 2, p. 233). Chicago, IL: Encyclopedia Brittanica.

Common Sense Media. (2010, November 19). Talking about "sexting." Retrieved August 3, 2012, from http://www.commonsensemedia.org

Crawford, K. (2009 August). Following you: Disciplines of listening in social media. Continuum: *Journal of Media & Cultural Studies, 23*, 525–535. doi: 10.1080/10304310903003270

The few, the proud, the women [Editorial]. (2012, July 13). *The New York Times*, p. A16. Retrieved August 8, 2012 from http://www.nytimes.com/2012/07/16/opinion/the-few-the-proud-the-women.html?_r=1&ref=editorials

YOUNG ADULTS AND SOCIAL MEDIA 11

Finin, T., Java, A., Joshi, A., Kale, A., Karandikar, A., & Kolari, P. (2008). The information ecology of social media and online communities. *AI Magazine, 29*(3), 77-92. Retrieved from http://go.galegroup.com

Greitemeyer, T., & Osswald, S. (2011). Playing prosocial video games increases the accessibility of prosocial thoughts. *The Journal Of Social Psychology, 151*(2), 121-128. doi:10.1080/00224540903365588

Lenhard, A., Purcell, K., Smith, A., & Zickuhr, K. (2010). Social media and mobile internet use among teens and young adults. *Pew Internet & American Life Project.* Retrieved from http://web.pewinternet.org

Madden, M., & Smith, A. (2010). Reputation management and social media. *Pew Internet & American Life Project.* Retrieved from http://ictlogy.net/bibliography/reports/projects.php?idp=1650

Rushkoff, D. & Dretzin, R (Writers) & Dretzin, R. (Producer). (2010). *Digital nation: Life on the virtual frontier* [Video file]. Retrieved August 8, 2012 from http://www.pbs.org/wgbh/pages/frontline/digitalnation/

Index

S

T

V

W

Made in the USA
Charleston, SC
24 July 2014